D0211196

THE WALL STREET JOURNAL
views
America tomorrow

THE WALL STREET JOURNAL
views
America
tomorrow

edited by Donald Moffitt

amacom

A Division of American Management Associations

Library of Congress Cataloging in Publication Data

Main entry under title:

The Wall Street journal views America tomorrow.

  Bibliography: p.
  1. United States—Civilization—1970-
—Miscellanea. 2. Twenty-first century—Forecasts.
I. Moffitt, Donald. II. The Wall Street Journal.
III. Title: America tomorrow.
E169.12.W34   973.92'08   76-52501
ISBN 0-8144-5438-0

Contents

Introduction

Introduction

In 1966, the *Wall Street Journal* began publishing a series of articles looking ahead to the year 2000. Reporters sought out knowledgeable people in many fields to sketch the most reasonable picture possible of life in America and elsewhere at the beginning of the third millenium. Ten years later, in 1976, the *Journal* reexamined that picture in another series of articles. The 1976 series forms the framework of this book. In addition, versions of a number of other major articles that deal with the future appear here.*

In some ways, the future is shaping up much as the experts predicted. Computers have become entrenched. The expected reduction in their size and relative cost is taking place, and concern over their use as impersonal monitors of private lives is growing. Instant satellite communications are, indeed, linking distant parts of the globe. If an ambitious space program has greatly shrunk because of its diminished glamour and increased cost, still America has put a spacecraft on Mars. Some military technology has advanced even faster than experts foresaw, although its cost has risen higher and faster than they thought too.

In other areas, including fundamental ones, the experts appear to have been wrong. This book focuses on these areas. To take an example from the chapter on population and the econ-

---

* A complete list of the articles involved appears at the end of this book.

1

omy, "78 million hypothetical Americans and a hypothetical $177 billion in yearly gross national product . . . appear simply to have vanished from America of the year 2000."

To many people, prophecy and prediction are vain pursuits. Columbia University's eminent futurist, Amitai Etzioni, recently chided his colleagues for their low esteem among the citizenry, and he challenged them to "tell us less about the year 2000, and more about 1978."

This book is not so futuristic. Though it reports predictions, it looks also at changes in expectations. In so doing, it attempts to identify those changes in the past ten years so profound that they seem likely to affect life a quarter of a century hence.

It appears that three major developments in the past decade have greatly affected the course of American society and have contributed the most to changing the expectations of many Americans. These developments arise from different causes, but their consequences are closely intertwined.

The first development was the energy crisis. For at least a century, low-cost energy had fueled a production revolution that enriched the world's industrial nations. Underlying the outlook for the gadget-cluttered world of 2000 that many futurists foresaw ten years ago was the assumption that energy would be readily available and cheap. Yet years before, in 1960, a notable Houston geologist, Michel Halbouty, was saying, "I can safely predict that between now and 1975 we will have an energy crisis in this country." Earlier, King Hubbert, another geologist, was predicting (rightly) that United States oil output would peak about 1970 and then decline. And by 1966, an obscure State Department official who had cultivated the confidence of some nearly-as-obscure Arab sheikhs was warning that the Arabs eventually would mix their oil with politics.

Where futurists went wrong was in their rash assumption that technology, in the form of abundant nuclear-power generation, would deftly step in to provide low-cost energy. Whatever else can be said about the source availability of energy in 2000, as the chapters on energy show, it will not be cheap.

If the economic limits of technology have become apparent in the energy field, they also appear to be nearing in other endeavors; and a widening awareness of the limits is a second major development that has affected expectations for the future. This awareness represents not so much a loss of "faith" in technology, though many people do question whether innovation necessarily improves the quality of life. Rather, the cost of fundamental technological advance, measured in environmental and health damage as well as actual money capital, increasingly is being perceived as prohibitive.

As a consequence, transportation experts, for example, now believe that the automobiles, airplanes, and railroads of the future will remain essentially unchanged, though they may become more fuel-efficient and in some cases more spartan and less comfortable than contemporary versions. Cost inflation has so greatly constrained technology that Pentagon futurists seriously question whether the nation will be able to afford some of the arms that it theoretically is capable of producing.

A third major development, which includes new skepticism toward progress that depends on technology, seems to have occurred in social and personal values. Ten years ago, the *Journal* article dealing with the American home of 2000 concerned itself almost exclusively with gadgetry and engineering. In another article, auto company prognosticators cheerfully described the five-car family garages of the future. Birthrates have declined so steeply in the past ten years, however, that the typical American family is unlikely to number anywhere near five people, much less own five cars.

Ten years ago the women's movement, quiescent for several generations, was only beginning its renaissance. And since then, major disruptions in the lives of many families have raised the question of the nuclear family's survival as a child-rearing unit. The qualified conclusion in the chapter on the family is that it will, in fact, survive. But the family's smaller size and its increasing vulnerability to more permissive alternatives in living and job arrangements now appear to be working at least as much change in American households as labor-saving devices ever could.

It should be emphasized that on major questions of food, energy, and world population, the views expressed in this book are not entirely optimistic. Nor are they universally accepted. Herman Kahn, for example, believes that "fears of a population explosion should disappear within the next half-century," and he thinks that "the population worries and alarmist exhortations of the 1960s and 1970s may well be recorded as an amusing episode in human history." Energy? "Except for temporary fluctuations caused by bad luck or poor management the world need not worry about energy shortages or costs in the future."*

The ground for Kahn's optimism is not fact, but faith—his faith in progress. In 6,000 or 7,000 years of civilization, this particular faith is a new one, dating back to the late seventeenth century. Before that, men commonly looked about them and saw a world in which life was short, brutish, and likely to remain so. Rationalism, technology, and cheap energy ultimately changed that view. But now, as even Kahn agrees, the world has reached a historic turning point. If so, some of the ideas that have governed men's affairs for the past several centuries may change radically. If foremost among the governing ideas was the idea of progress, we cannot be so certain that it will continue to prevail.

---

* Herman Kahn, *The Next 200 Years: A Scenario for America and the World.* New York: William Morrow and Company, 1976.

I
PEOPLE
Values and Lifestyles

1

America: Its People and Economy in 2000

"There's not much interest in long-range forecasts around here any more," Mark Kendall said early in 1976. "We've been wrong too often." Kendall is an economist at the National Planning Association, in Washington, a research group that undertakes a variety of forecasting chores for government and business. His observation suggests his frustration with the apparent futility of some of his work. Ten years earlier, the NPA was busy on a major study for the government to determine just how big and prosperous the United States would be in the year 2000. Today, the NPA forecast seems, to put it charitably, most unlikely to materialize. Indeed, it seems so far off that analysts like Kendall are reluctant to make any long-range forecasts.

Why have the most painstaking, sophisticated forecasts proved so unsatisfactory? And how, ten years closer to the year 2000, does the economy now appear to be shaping up? The questions loom large in the calculations of long-range planners in government and in private business. Although other factors play a part, forecasters generally agree that the answers to both questions lie in the country's recent surprising changes in population trends. For various reasons, the population has grown far less rapidly than almost anyone imagined ten years ago. And it probably will keep growing at a minuscule rate. Because population estimates for the year 2000 must be sharply revised, so must estimates of the economy's size and shape. The striking consequence: 78 million hypothetical Americans and a hypothetical $177 billion in yearly gross national product (at 1960 prices) appear simply to have vanished from America of the year 2000.

In 1966, NPA analysts foresaw a gross national product in the year 2000 of $2,280 billion in 1960 prices. In 1976, a similar estimate by Department of Commerce analysts projected $2,103 billion. Even this lower figure may turn out much too high, many economists think. The difference in forecasts is huge. The GNP for 1975, in 1960 prices, was about $815 billion, so the $180 billion reduction in estimate amounts to about one-fifth of all the goods and services that Americans turned out in 1975.

When the NPA made its study, United States population in the year 2000 seemed likely to reach nearly 340 million. The projection assumed that women on the average would each bear 3.1 children. But women have had fewer children. Contraception and abortion have become widespread. A long severe recession, together with corrosive inflation rates, has burdened household finances and deterred some couples from having children. Other developments, ranging from the desire of many women to make careers outside the home to widespread worry over environmental pollution, apparently have also worked against parenthood.

Consequently, it now appears that the average American woman will bear only 2.1 children in her lifetime instead of 3.1. If the trend continues, the population in the year 2000 will reach only 262 million instead of the 340 million projected earlier. The increase is still large; the population in early 1976 was only 214 million. But the lowered birthrate already tells us that more than 12 million Americans who had been expected to exist in early 1976, don't; the decade-earlier forecast projected 226 million people in 1975.

The number of Americans in the year 2000 could be, in fact, even fewer than now foreseen. The smallest of three estimates recently made by the Department of Commerce was only 245 million. Many economists and other analysts think this figure may turn out to be the most accurate. The impact of contraception, abortion, and other developments, these experts say, has yet to be fully reflected in birthrates. "The possible effects of all these factors have not been subjected to comprehensive analysis," a Department of Commerce study conceded.* The point is important. A department analyst observes: "If our population estimate for 2000 turns out to be much too high, and that possibility certainly can't be dismissed, estimates covering such economic matters as the size of the GNP in 2000 are bound to prove excessive as well."

If Americans begin living a good deal longer, the rate of population growth might appreciably rise. The Department of Commerce study suggests that "a breakthrough in the control of major chronic diseases (such as cancer) could lead to substantial reductions in mortality rates. If such breakthroughs occur, the future population of the United States could be somewhat larger and could have a significantly older age structure" than now seems likely.†

Even without such advances, the population will grow older. In contrast to today, most Americans in the year 2000 will be more than thirty years old. People between thirty-five and fifty-five years of age, those born in the 1956-1965 baby boom, will account for nearly 16 percent of the population, up from less than 11 percent in 1976.

People younger than thirty-five and people between fifty-five and sixty-four will make up smaller proportions of the population than they do now. The citizens who will be nearly sixty-five were born during the second stage of the Depression, when the birthrate was unusually low. Improved medical care and a somewhat higher birthrate among black Americans could help raise the black proportion of the population to nearly 14 percent in 2000 from just under 12 percent today.

Many people welcome the downward revisions in popula-

* Bureau of the Census, "Projections of the Population of the United States: 1975 to 2050," *Current Population Reports*, Series P-25, No. 601, October 1975.

† *Ibid.*

tion and economic growth. The *Wall Street Journal's* series of articles on the year 2000 ten years ago took 340 million Americans as the probable population and called the prospect of overcrowding "horrifying." Clearly, the prospect of only 262 million people is a good deal less so. To many people, economic growth divorced from any advance in the quality of life seems, over the past decade, to have become distasteful. Indeed, the opinion that economic growth may reflect an increasingly brutish life has become entrenched.

Oskar Morgenstern, the New York University economist, expresses this view. "Anything that leads to a transaction in monetary form, where goods and services change hands against money, enters GNP," he says. "To wit: If we are stuck in one of the thousands of traffic jams, if airplanes are stacked and cannot land on schedule, if fires break out and other disasters occur that require repair—up goes the GNP!"

Like the lowered population forecast of 262 million, the lowered GNP forecast of $2,103 billion for the year 2000 may be too high. If the population fails to reach 262 million, GNP almost certainly will fall below the new forecast. Even if the population does reach 262 million, GNP may fall below the new forecast. The lower GNP estimate is grounded in several assumptions that may be overstated. One assumption is that unemployment in the year 2000 will amount to only 4 percent of the labor force, in contrast to the 7-plus percent rate of early 1976. Another and perhaps even more questionable assumption is that labor productivity, the per-worker output of goods and services, will keep rising at an annual rate of about 3 percent.

If 3 percent seems modest, keep in mind that such an increase means a doubling in only a quarter of a century. On the average, productivity in private enterprise has risen at about that rate since the Second World War. But this rate may be unsustainable. Historically, it is an anomaly. Between 1899 and 1914, productivity rose only 1.5 percent a year. Between 1914 and 1928, it rose only 2.5 percent a year.

If the calculations of many economists are correct, capital increasingly will be channeled into controlling pollution rather than increasing output. Services businesses and government, in which it is difficult to increase productivity, will continue to expand. Employee demand for more leisure time and employee opposition to anything smacking of production speedups are expected to continue. The size and shape of the economy in 2000 depend on other imponderables: inflation, for one. High rates of inflation have tended to limit economic growth, or so economists generally agree, because investors shy from risking long-term capital that will be returned in depreciated dollars. Ever since the Second World War, public and private debt have risen steeply, stimulating economic growth. In the years ahead, this outstanding debt may, on balance, burden the economy.

Some students believe that the fast-growing cost of providing more generously for more older people, especially in the Social Security system, may tend to impoverish working people. Still other imponderables range from the cost and availability of energy to America's relations with poorer countries. Their economic aspirations and their populations will continue to rise. Small wonder that Leonard L. Fischman, an analyst at Resources for the Future, concludes that long-range forecasting "is an art and not a statistical procedure."

Fischman's nonprofit, Washington-based organization recently made an analysis that attempted to accommodate the wide range of possibilities that could affect America on the road to the year 2000. The analysis envisioned four different broad patterns, spanning relatively high and relatively low growth in basic factors like population and labor productivity. On the high side, the GNP in the year 2000 was put at $2,600 billion, some $500 billion above the current projection by the Department of Commerce. On the low side, the GNP might hit only $1,900 billion, or $200 billion under the government's projection.

The implications for long-range planners and forward-thinking managers are clear. No longer can they uncritically accept as assumptions the growth-rate factors of the recent past.

2

Corporate Futurists

Joseph L. Shapiro spends a good deal of time in his sunny office in the planning department of the Gillette Company in Boston contemplating how women's changing role will change the family of the future. He is not sure what that has to do with selling razor blades. No matter. As Gillette's resident crystal-ball gazer, he is paid not to answer questions but simply to raise them.

Shapiro's title at Gillette is Director of Commercial Research. Less formally but perhaps more accurately, he is called a futurist. He and other futurists are being employed by companies like Shell Oil Corporation, American Telephone and Telegraph Company, and General Electric Corporation to discern the future implications of current trends.

One knowledgeable consultant on future studies is James B. Webber, a director of the Cambridge Research Institute in Cambridge, Massachusetts. He believes that as many as one out of five of the five hundred largest American companies employ futurists—men and women who "play the genie in a practical sense, keeping firms abreast so they don't get caught short."

The energy crisis, wage and price controls, the environmental outcry—such traumas caught many a corporate management off-balance, and the experience has persuaded them that it might not be a bad idea to establish a resident Cassandra. "Times are perilous," observed Wayne Boucher, then secretary of The Futures Group, a research and consulting firm in Connecticut. "For management, it's a crisis with a capital C. And the changes will accelerate."

The corporate planning departments usually responsible for management's tentative ventures into futurism appear to be far from adequate. Typically, a planning-department project involved the analysis of economic data, marketing statistics, and demographic profiles to estimate the market and profit potential of a new product, usually over a span of no more than five years. "It looked at birthrates without considering birth-control pills," Boucher says.

Futurists try to peer as far as thirty years ahead. They try to evaluate the influence of a host of social and political factors on corporate problems. Usually, futurists are professionally trained as economists or market researchers. But many of them appear to have transcended the conventional boundaries of their specialties to become voracious readers of all kinds of general and technical literature, brain-pickers of other creative professionals, and canny trend-spotters themselves. Their work no longer is called corporate planning. In some companies it is social and political forecasting. In others, it is environmental scanning. And in still others, futurists are engaged in the design of "early warning systems."

Similarly, the futurist's place in the organization chart varies considerably from company to company. At Shell Oil, a team of six futurists works within a forty-member planning department. At American Telephone and Telegraph's planning division, eight staffers with an "artistic temperament" or a background in history, literature, or journalism work alongside forty economists and statisticians to help widen and deepen the planning perspective.

Still, futurists generally have no real authority. They are wont to be wily in the ways they make their points to top management. One futurist often sneaks his ideas into speeches that he ghost-writes for executives, in the hope that the executives will absorb the ideas and treat them as their own. He also builds qualitative forecasts from hard economic data in the belief that executives will readily understand and accept projections derived from hard figures.

Gillette's Shapiro is adept at friendly persuasion. "He employs it so subtly that often people aren't even aware he's persuading them," a Gillette executive says. "Sometimes they think they've come up with the ideas themselves."

Born in 1913, Shapiro worked as a social and statistical researcher for the Social Security Administration and as a market researcher for several companies. Among them was the old Toni division, now the personal care division, of Gillette. In 1968 he was asked by Vincent C. Ziegler, Gillette's chairman and chief executive officer, to join the planning department. He is its long-term seer; four other staffers deal largely with specific short-term projects.

Shapiro's own maiden venture was a report outlining the prospects and perils the company might encounter by the year 2000. Along the way, he found, the company would have to consider entry into the service industry. A stabilizing growth rate in population, he reasoned, would translate into a declining rate of growth in new products. A few years later, Gillette took its first cautious steps into the service industry. It acquired Welcome Wagon International Inc. in 1971 and Jafra Cosmetics Inc. (whose beauty consultants supply cosmetics at the homes of consumers) in 1973.

"We made the decisions largely on the basis of Joe's information," Ziegler says. "Both businesses are doing well. And by 1980, service should be a significant part of our business."

Ziegler sometimes assigns Shapiro to take part in acquisition discussions so that, in the presence of Gillette executives, he can raise pertinent questions about the potential of a prospective acquisition. Management at other times directs specific questions to Shapiro. What, for example, do changing age categories in the American population imply for Gillette? In this case, Shapiro responded that the company should begin to design and market products for consumers older than fifty-five, a group it had been largely ignoring.

Shapiro is continuing to revise his report on the year 2000.

From the three newspapers he reads each day and the thirty or forty magazines he reads each month, he gleans clues to trends. He talks to colleagues and other professionals to determine the likely significance of these trends. A question he has asked: If it is true that fewer families take their meals together than in the past, does this mean that sales of formal dinnerware will decline?

Shapiro rarely interviews outsiders in sensitive areas lest he reveal Gillette's interest in a new market. "Like the Lady of Shalott," he says, "I know the outside world from a mirror. I read and read and read, and at some point I come through the critical mass, the facts either filling in or disclaiming my hypothesis." A typical hypothesis: The structure of the family will be profoundly affected by women's liberation.

Futurists like Shapiro cannot provide specific answers to the questions raised by their hypotheses. They believe, however, that the questions will be valid if the hypotheses are carefully examined. Their questions often come in "What if?" form. "Presenting alternatives gets executives to do 'What-if' thinking," says Ian Wilson, a futurist at General Electric since 1967. "If that's the only way to forecast now, and it is, so be it. We simply can't do without it."

Wilson first involved himself in "What-if" thinking in 1967, when he did a general study of the future that failed to take into account the possibility of widespread student rioting. It occurred just one year later. Reviewing conversations with sources he had interviewed, Wilson became aware that they had mentioned all the factors that precipitated the riots. They were, in fact, predictable. "We learned that we had to see trends in synoptic and interacting modes, not in isolation," Wilson says.

About the same time, Wilson began asking "What-if" questions about the minority-rights movement. What if, he asked, the movement spread to that put-upon and discriminated-against group called women? A year before the federal government required affirmative action in women's employment, General Electric had prepared its own guidelines to equal-opportunity employment for women as a consequence of the question that Wilson posed.

Recently, Wilson has been raising questions about energy consumption in the 1980s. What if consumers are still deeply concerned over energy conservation? It implies, of course, that General Electric should pursue energy efficiency as a long-term strategy as well as a short-term marketing tactic.

General Electric many years ago became one of the first major American corporations to take futurism seriously and make an earnest commitment to it. Neither Shell Oil nor American Telephone and Telegraph created social and political forecasting units until 1972. In that year each hired teams of individuals with divergent expertise. In Shell's case, the company was simply responding to the possibility of becoming more dependent on foreign crude oil. "Future shock hit us," says René Zentner, manager of the Shell team. "As the world changed, we realized we couldn't continue to follow constant trends and count on a 5 percent annual growth rate."

Shell's futurists are Zentner, two economists, a lawyer, a master of business administration, and a sociologist. Each pursues his own project. The lawyer, for example, is trying to project energy policy. The business-school graduate is analyzing political and economic trends abroad.

American Telephone and Telegraph has organized its future studies differently. "Working separately sets up artificial barriers," says Henry Boettinger, director of corporate planning. Thus the planning division's eight futurists closely work with economists and statisticians in a handful of special areas. Trends in regulation is one of them.

The life insurance industry has used its own trade organization, the Institute of Life Insurance, to create a think tank. Coordinated by the institute's Edith Weiner, the program, begun in 1970, employs ninety volunteers from the institute's two hundred member-firms. The volunteers monitor sixty publications each month to supply material for thrice-yearly "Trend Analysis Reports" covering developments in science and technology, social sciences, business, economics, politics, and government.

Material selected by the volunteers goes to a committee of executives who organize each report. One recent report, "The Life Cycle," explored the possibility that the conventional pattern of many people's lives, involving formal education followed by work followed by retirement, could give way to a less structured system. This led Bankers Life Company in Des Moines to design, for possible future sale, a "life cycle" policy with premiums scaled in a kind of proportion to the insured's earnings status. Another report gave executives of Equitable Life Assurance Society in New York the idea for a marketing program aimed at two-income families. "Agencies never approached women before," says Anna Rappaport, vice president and associate actuary for marketing at Equitable. "But now families need insurance on both spouses."

Such "human values" have become increasingly significant in the view of Richard Davis, a futurist for Whirlpool Corporation. Davis gained fame in the 1960s as a technological forecaster. He predicted the introduction of permanent-press fabrics and enabled Whirlpool to reach the market first with washers and dryers designed to accommodate those materials. Davis is still keeping a close eye on technological advance. But he says that the growing number of working mothers, fewer children, and reliance on paper rather than cloth could change the market for washers and dryers as much as any technological advance. "Anyone who ignores these factors," he says, "does so at his own peril."

3

The Family of the Future

The American family, fractured by divorce, bewildered by
sexual freedom, threatened by women's liberation, and seemingly scorned by its progeny, is going to make it. By the year
2000, the nuclear family, the group of father, mother, and dependent children that has been the dominant family form in
the West since the eighteenth century, will not only be around
but will be a more benevolent institution than many people
think it has been.

Such is the consensus of psychologists, theologians, counselors, sociologists, and others who make a business of studying family life. They think that the family of the future will be
smaller, less permanent, and more vulnerable to change, but
that it will survive and even thrive. Virginia Satir, an influen-
tial author and family therapist in Palo Alto, California, says of
the family twenty-four years hence: "I see a freedom without
anarchy. I see people becoming more mature and a whole new
change in how men and women can be in touch with themselves." A few blocks away at the Mental Research Institute,
Stanford University psychologist Paul Watzlawick says,
"Within a generation, we shall be back at an extremely
family-oriented society."

One of the most striking changes in the family of the year 2000 involves the woman's role. She will emerge, or so it seems, as a full partner and breadwinner, as indeed she already is doing; 7.4 percent of wives earned more money than their husbands in a 1969 census survey, half again as many as outearned hubby in a 1959 sample. Out of this will flow other changes. Families will be smaller. Ways of life will be more diverse. For some people this will mean greater personal fulfillment. For others it will mean greater instability and divorce.

On the surface, current trends do not appear to favor the continued existence of the family. Married couples now are divorcing at nearly twice the rate of the 1950s. Escalating divorce is prevalent throughout Western society. Roughly one in every three American marriages now ends in divorce. Younger people are shying away from early marriage and often choose to live together unmarried. The number of single people between the ages of twenty-five and thirty-four who have never been married jumped by 50 percent from 1970 to 1975, the Bureau of Census reports. A straw in the wind? The housing authority of Portland, Oregon, recently decided to permit unmarried couples to apply for subsidized housing.

Stresses on the family structure and moral upheavals are probably more evident in California than elsewhere. It has long been a haven for the restless and rootless. Marin County, a well-to-do suburban area of San Francisco, recorded more divorces than marriages in 1975. At the Family Service Agency of San Francisco, a private counseling service, a survey recently disclosed that nearly 7 percent of couples seeking help were in unmarried "living-together arrangements," or, in the jargon of counseling, "LTAs." "That's up from zero percent three years ago," says Lyle Slaughter, director of counseling for the agency.

But marriage still booms. Roughly 75 percent of divorced women and 80 percent of divorced men remarry, census figures show. "We're in a terribly overmarried society," anthropologist Margaret Mead observed in a 1971 article, "because we can't think of any other way for anybody to live, except in matrimony as couples. . . . Everybody gets married—and unmarried—and married, but they're all married to somebody most of the time."*

Among Catholics, the lure of matrimony remains so strong that it often overcomes the stigma of excommunication. The Reverend James Young, a Paulist priest and theologian in Cambridge, Massachusetts, is a leader of a movement to bring divorced and remarried Catholics back into the fold. He says, "I think it is quite likely" that by the end of the century the church will abandon the dogma that subjects a divorced and remarried Catholic to excommunication. Even now, he says, it is rarely enforced. "More and more people in second marriages are continuing to live as Catholics," he says.

Father Young thinks that "at least half of divorced Catholics remarry now." He thinks the divorce rate shows that "people are looking for more satisfaction in marriage" and no longer will remain tolerant of the prospect of lifelong unhappiness. This amounts, he thinks, to a "twentieth-century revolution," ultimately leading to less divorce as couples "marry late in life, more wisely, and more committed." Meanwhile, the very prevalence of divorce is making life easier for divorced people. "You're not a leper if you're divorced now," observes Bernard R. O'Brien, executive director of the Family and Children's Service agency in Kansas City.

Sociologists like Arlie Hochschild at the University of California in Berkeley think that people are "moving toward a two-stage marriage." In the first phase, she says, they "live together and figure out if they like each other. In the second, they legally marry and commit themselves to a family."

That family will be smaller; recent and current trends in birthrates nearly dictate it. "We are witnessing today a clearly marked transition from a three-child to a two-child family norm," says William Burke, an economist at the Federal Reserve Bank of San Francisco. Even the Catholic Church, Father Young thinks, will move toward recognition of the "childless marriage" as a legitimate choice in a world otherwise threatened by population pressures.

* "The Future of the Family," *Barnard Alumnae Magazine*, Winter 1971 (New York: Barnard College).

Smaller families subject to more frequent breakups will be of major economic significance for many industries, especially housing. "The single-family detached home is definitely going to decline by the year 2000," says Robert Sheehan, director of economic research for the National Association of Home Builders. "I'd guess [it will amount] to 20 percent to 30 percent by the end of the century," against 50 percent to 60 percent of all housing begun in recent years, he says.

Even in the suburbs, where most Americans will live in the year 2000, builders will turn more to apartments and townhouses for smaller families to keep down the cost of land and construction. "The average home will still be three bedrooms," Sheehan says, "but you'll see more two bedrooms."

Promoted and debated for generations, family planning is a reality in America today. The speed at which it has become a reality has confounded demographers and others trying to foretell the future. Until recently, America was one of the more fertile nations on earth. In 1900, the average family had nearly five children. At that time, in a rural society, large families meant welcome hands. Now, children are an economic burden.

Even so, some experts detect a slight rise in the birthrate in California that could portend a baby boom of sorts in the future. The key to family size may lie in the extent to which women seek and find careers outside the home. Nearly half of all grown women have jobs now, up from one-third twenty-five years ago. Many mothers of school-age children are pushing for day-care centers and seeking other ways to manage children and careers simultaneously.

To other stresses on marriage, the competing careers of husband and wife will continue to contribute. Yet the work force will include an increasing number of married couples who always have had working careers. Helen Tinsley, a supervisor at the San Francisco Family Service Agency, thinks many of these couples will undertake written or unwritten agreements on the division of housework and child care, family relocation for career reasons, and other important issues. More couples, too, may give up their own housework. "I look for traditional household responsibilities to be taken over more and more by specialists such as professional housecleaners, and virtually all women to be absorbed into the work force," says Ivan Nye, a Washington State University sociologist. Today, he says, an estimated 57 percent of American mothers of school-age children work at some time during the year. He thinks this majority will increase.

Some traditionalists are rather disturbed by all this. "It bothers me," says William Burke, the Federal Reserve Bank economist. "My wife stayed home and gave our one child, a boy, her undivided attention through high school. It gave him some stability." Others think that men will come to enjoy more of their families' domestic lives as their wives share more of the financial burden. "Men will be able to relax, and that could ease tensions in the family," says Lyle Slaughter of San Francisco Family Service. Having fewer children will benefit men as well as women, Margaret Mead believes. "Nobody looks at father and thinks what a life he'd have if he hadn't had those five children," she has written. "He might have been able to paint instead of being a stock broker. Or [be] a musician instead of running a jewelry store he inherited."*

Sociologists and others continue to ponder the implications of the more extreme lifestyles that emerged in the 1960s, especially in the West. Thousands of couples, married and unmarried, sought fulfillment in communes, group marriage, "swinging" or so-called recreational sex, and other unconventional behavior.

But many authorities observe that the communal movement, at least, is as old as America itself. They do not think it is growing significantly. And it may in fact be shrinking. "Most ex-members say that communes are for losers now," Slaughter finds. John H. Weakland, a clinical anthropologist at the Mental Research Institute, says, "I don't see how the utopian emphasis can be sustained indefinitely. Communal movements and group marriages don't get away from old problems."

Nonetheless, various forms of open marriage allowing each partner greater freedom to engage in outside relationships, even sexual relationships, may flourish, many students of fam-

* *Ibid.*

ily life believe. Open marriage, like the communal movement, is hardly an innovation of the 1960s. What is new, perhaps, is the self-conscious organization with which some Americans have promoted it.

Jonathan and Bunny Dana, filmmakers who jointly produced a recent X-rated documentary movie called *Sandstone,* are advocates of open marriage. Jonathan Dana, twenty-nine in 1976, has a doctorate in organizational behavior and a master's degree in business administration from Stanford. He and his twenty-eight-year-old wife, Bunny, moved into Sandstone, a commune for married couples in Southern California, in the early seventies. There they learned about swinging on a grand scale. "In having an intimate relationship outside marriage," Bunny Dana says, "so many of the questions of ownership and mutual needs are crystallized." After two years, the Danas left Sandstone. Now they are living with another couple "in what some people might call a group marriage," Jonathan Dana says. "I don't think the nuclear family is passé," he adds, "but there are a lot of different styles of living. It will be increasingly more common for people to live the way they want to, communally, in homosexual marriages, or whatever. American culture is great at co-opting change."

On that same score, some experts believe that variant marriage forms are merely becoming more open and not more prevalent than in the past. In any case, professionals in family welfare doubt that such forms would benefit most conventionally married couples. "Jealousy is just as alive in any kind of experimentation as it was in grandma's time," says Bernard O'Brien of the Kansas City family and children's agency. "When you come right down to it, there is hardly anyone who can stand to share a loved person."

In the view of some experts, open marriage is simply one element in a whole syndrome, including the expansion of day care for children and the increasing divorce rate, that threatens the nuclear family. On the other hand, they think a still-unobtrusive trend may work toward making family life more stable than it is now. This is the aging of the American population. The Bureau of Census estimates that by the year 2020, Americans over sixty-five years of age will nearly double in

number to about 43 million from 22 million today. Because
people will live longer and presumably in better health, says
Vern Bengston, a sociologist at the California Institute of
Technology, more children may know their grandparents better. And more people in their middle years, their forties and
fifties, will have parents or grandparents to whom to turn for
emotional support even if they live apart. "Once grandma has
raised the children, she spends a lot of time keeping track of
what everyone in the family is doing," Bengston says. "This
can be very valuable with increasing divorce rates . . . because grandma is a stabilizing factor."

But will grandma become a swinger? Increasingly, either
spontaneously or with the encouragement of counselors or
others, elderly people appear to be experimenting with ways
of living that include sexual liaisons. Bengston knows of a
seventy-three-year-old woman and a seventy-year-old man,
both widowed, who lived a few doors apart and carried on a
secret affair. "No one in the family could understand why she
bought a king-size bed after her husband died," he says.
"They had a playful courtship, something neither had in forty
years of marriage."

4
Women at Work

The personnel placement order is simple enough. A new assembly-line inspector is needed, someone who is reliable, works at a steady pace, and is unlikely to quit in the middle of a production push; someone who will be willing also to shoulder managerial responsibility when the pressure is on. In the old days, the solution would have been simple enough, too: hire a man. Today, the answer is more frequently to hire a woman. As Betty Friedan puts it, "The cliché of women's absenteeism and turnover isn't valid anymore."

Male chauvinists may accuse Betty Friedan of having an ax to grind. Yet employers increasingly have found that the characterization of a working woman as a flighty factor in the work force is invalid. Quit rates, turnover, and absenteeism among women are dropping not only in comparison with levels of past years but also in some cases when measured against levels for male employees.

All this may not be apparent in figures kept by the Department of Labor. The department has not broken down quit rates—rates of employee-initiated departures—according to sex since 1968. Records kept by corporations, however, show that women are staying on the job longer. At the American

Telephone and Telegraph Company, for example, female turnover rates in the first quarter of 1974 fell to 11.5 percent from 19.6 percent in the first quarter of 1971. Male turnover for the period also dropped, but less strikingly, to 5.1 percent from 7 percent. At General Motors Corporation, female quit rates, though still higher than male, shrank to 4.7 percent in 1973 from 5.3 percent in 1972; the rate of quitting among male employees rose to 2.3 percent from 1.9 percent over the same period.

Polaroid Corporation said in 1974 that its turnover rate was highest in lower-level jobs and that "men in those slots now show exactly the same turnover rates as women." At Aetna Life and Casualty Company, the turnover rate for women in technical, managerial, and professional jobs worked out at 8.3 percent in 1973, compared with 11 percent for men in those kinds of jobs.

The underlying reasons for these changes are diverse. Economic factors, including the specters of inflation and high unemployment, have made employees of both sexes reluctant to leave their jobs. Still, much of the improvement in the stability of women on the job traces back to a period before the recent recession. Many corporate executives agree that a change in corporate attitudes toward women has been an important factor. Indeed, such executives are coming around to the belief long advanced by women: that unreliability and job-hopping are related more to job satisfaction, salary, occupational level, and age than to sex. Employers, whether under pressure or on their own, have been treating women workers better, and the women have been responding. Says Donald L. Liebers, director of human resources and development at AT&T: "Women have long been a stabilizing force here, but that's increasing now with their additional opportunities." Says Paul Armknecht, a Department of Labor economist: "Women are no longer under pressure to leave the labor force. Thus they're more permanently attached than in the past."

The enhancement of benefits, especially for maternity, is one improvement in the lot of what used to be called the working girl. When Noreen Haffner had her first child in 1971, she had to take an unpaid leave from Southern New England

Telephone Company at the end of her seventh month of pregnancy. That was what the company policy required. In 1973, Haffner had her second child. She left her job at the telephone company on a Friday, gave birth the next Wednesday and returned to work four weeks later. Although she received no disability pay, she said she was "much more satisfied with the corporate policy the second time. I don't think it hurt me, my baby, or my job."

Women themselves have forced some change in the corporate attitude. No longer willing to take a backseat to their male co-workers, women have brought legal pressure to bear on corporate employers. Although some executives assert altruistic motives for their bettering of women's job conditions, the fact remains that failure to improve them could lead to expensive lawsuits from unhappy women workers.

Family trends have played a part, too. Shirley Johnson, professor of economics at Vassar College, says the high divorce rate has put many women as the head of their household and these women "won't be in and out of the labor force as much." Then too, pregnancy rates have dropped. And Elizabeth Koontz, formerly of the Women's Bureau in the Department of Labor, observes that working mothers with small children have easier access to outside child care than in the past. All this has encouraged women, once having found a job, to stick with it.

Some steadfast women employees stick with it for a negative reason, however. They say they stay put, even when they are unhappy, because of discrimination in the job market. A chemist with RCA Corporation contends that she has not been eager to look for another job because "few companies are willing to hire a female chemist; it's traditionally a male position." Despite advances into the executive suite, many women say they are not being recruited by executive headhunters. "Executive search firms are very sexist," says a female manager at Aetna. "They reflect the sexism of their clients."

Or at least some of them may. Millie McCoy, a vice-president of the New York recruiting firm of Handy Associates Inc., says that "most of our clients have gone out of their way to find minorities, women, or other 'protected classes.' And once they've hired them in supervisory positions, the old stereotypes disappear."

Certainly, times are changing. And as stereotypes are shattering, women are taking notice.

Merle Daniel, a special correspondent for United Services Automobile Association, based in San Antonio, has taken three insurance courses for which her insurance-company employer paid after she passed them. "The benefits have made this job more attractive to me," she says. "I've considered working other places, but I've remained here because it seems more advantageous to stay." Mildred May, manager of the business office for a New England concern, left the company in 1947 to raise her two daughters. She returned in 1965 and has held several managerial positions. "The first time around," she says of her job history, "what incentive did a woman have? She knew she was going to be a secretary or stenographer. Now, the sky's the limit."

5

Gains for Gay Liberation

Some employers have made a cautious but noticeable change in their policy on the employment of homosexuals. Although overt homosexuality often remains a barrier to employment or advancement, many companies have recently begun to indicate, quietly, that they no longer regard private sexual activity as a corporate concern. "It's a matter of dealing with reality in a pluralistic society," the personnel director of an insurance company observes. "As long as the individual keeps his or her personal life as his or her personal life, it doesn't influence our decisions."

It is true that few corporate employers are eager to publicize their new tolerance. "We're at the point where a number of businesses have openly hired and used gays," says Ron Gold, a spokesman for a homosexual organization called the National Gay Task Force, "but we're not yet to the point where they're bragging about this minority." David Whitsett, an industrial psychologist, says that "discrimination is becoming less and less respectable but homosexuality will be the last employment barrier to fall."

It is also true that the changes in policy and practice have occurred largely in major urban areas with large homosexual

29

populations and a tradition of toleration. "It's appropriate for New York," a personnel director says of the changing attitude toward homosexuals, "but I'm led to believe it's still too sensitive" in many other places. The barriers are being lowered mainly in service industries, such as insurance companies, brokerage firms, and advertising agencies, rather than in manufacturing companies.

Some retailers have been among the most tolerant employers. A few years ago, Michael McPherson, a senior merchandising specialist at a big New York department store, appeared on a local television news program and declared his homosexuality. That did not prevent the store, a year later, from promoting him to a manager's job in his furniture department. "We'll see some dramatic changes," McPherson predicts of homosexual employment in the future.

Male and female homosexuals alike have been accepted increasingly by employers. Some executives think that lesbianism may be more readily tolerated; it is less threatening, they say, to male employers. Also, most lesbians are less visible than many male homosexuals.

While the courts have not come down squarely on the side of homosexuals in employment issues, legal rulings have tended toward toleration. Federal courts, for example, have required that a connection be established between an individual's conduct and his or her performance on the job in order to justify discrimination toward a homosexual. In effect, this appears to assert that homosexuality in itself is not a sufficient ground for dismissing an employee. Anthony Mondello, general counsel for the Civil Service Commission, has put it this way: "The courts have told us, 'You fellows aren't anointed and shouldn't be making moral judgments.' And I think that's a reasonable position for the government to be in."

Court decisions have encouraged civil-rights laws and ordinances granting homosexuals equal opportunity in employment, housing, and public accommodation. Between 1972 and 1974, homosexual rights ordinances were passed in Ann Arbor, Michigan; Berkeley, California; Columbus, Ohio; Detroit and East Lansing, Michigan; Minneapolis, San Francisco, Seattle, Toronto, and Washington, D.C. None of the other legislation is as comprehensive as the Washington ordinance, and enforcement in most cases has remained spotty. But homosexual libertarians see such ordinances as a foot in the door, anyway. Says Frank Kameny, president of the homosexual Mattachine Society in Washington: "I've been in the movement for twelve years and used to imagine in my daydreams that there would be civil-rights laws for gay people. I'm still surprised at their reception."

The 1973 decision of the American Psychiatric Association to remove homosexuality from its catalog of mental disorders, and its conclusion that homosexuality implies no general personality impairment, have given a rationale to legislation. Activism of homosexual organizations, too, has made them a political force. The number of homosexual organizations grew from 20 in 1969 to 1,400 in 1974, according to a count by the Gay Activist Alliance in New York. "The social dynamics of tolerance have grown," says Morty Manford, president of the alliance.

Laws against sodomy and other "crimes against nature" have become a major target of these groups. Harold Weiner, a New York lawyer who has defended homosexuals in the courts, says, "As these acts are decriminalized, it removes the stigma from the homosexual's mind, and from the employer's, about hiring a criminal. After all, nobody fires a corporate executive for having an affair with his secretary."

In 1973, the Northwestern Bell Telephone Company in Minneapolis declined to hire a job applicant who admitted that he was a homosexual. "Until society recognizes homosexuality as socially acceptable behavior, we believe that employing known homosexuals would tend to have an adverse effect on how our company is regarded by other employees and the general public," the company explained. In 1974, the Minneapolis city council enacted a homosexual-rights ordinance. Northwestern Bell then changed its position. The company, a spokesman said, "will of course comply with the ordinance, and though it is confined to Minneapolis, we will make it uniform throughout our employment offices elsewhere in the state."

Another Minneapolis firm, Honeywell Inc., had been the

target of homosexual protests because of allegedly discriminatory hiring policies. In 1970, a Honeywell vice president had written a letter stating that "we wouldn't employ a known homosexual. Our practice is the result of actual adverse prior experience." Later, the company acknowledged that it had changed its policy in "a reversal from the point of view stated in the letter. It's more in tune with the feeling of the times."

"There's a great consciousness of the need for nondiscrimination in all areas because of practical considerations. There are so many enforcement agencies watching to right wrongs," says George Burns, formerly a vice president of Trans World Airlines Inc.

But a few firms have even exploited employee homosexuality. Cinema 5 Ltd. in New York hired Vito Russo from the Museum of Modern Art specifically to market films to homosexual audiences. "They knew I was gay when they hired me," Russo says. "They not only realized that it's okay to hire gay people, but that there's a gay market to be reached." In San Francisco, a beer distributor hired a homosexual to sell to gay bars.

More typical is the attitude of a New York City bank, Manufacturers Hanover Trust Company. William Bahlman, then a clerk at the bank, told his supervisor he could not work overtime because he wanted to attend homosexual rallies and meetings. Bahlman recalls that his superior "told me he personally thought it was disgusting, but that it wasn't any of his business, so long as I didn't embarrass the bank." Bahlman later was promoted by the bank.

One of the few firms to have enacted a written policy toward homosexuality by 1974 was Pacific Telephone and Telegraph Company. The policy declares that "an employee with a homosexual orientation wouldn't be terminated solely for that orientation." A company spokesman says, "If someone came in for a job and was militantly gay, we'd reject them—not because they're militantly gay, but because their apparent mode of life would hardly be consistent with job performance."

If business has been conservative in acknowledging homosexuality, the professions have been less so. There are organizations for homosexual doctors, psychologists, and academics. A homosexual employment and counseling service in New York tries to place openly homosexual job hunters with nondiscriminatory employers. Still, homosexuals have a long way to go before dissipating the hostility toward them. As Manford of the Gay Activist Alliance puts it, "Psychiatrists tell us we're sick; churches tell us we're sinners; capitalists call us subversives; Communists tell us we're decadent. This has taken its toll on people and their ability to recognize the humanity of one-tenth of the population."

6

Two-Career Couples

Sharon Baum, as assistant vice president and manager of advertising for Chemical Bank in New York, tightly schedules her time. Index cards listing every chore she has to get done run her life. It always seems to Baum, who was thirty-five years old in 1975, that her list is a lot longer than her day. "Every single minute is taken up," she says. "I never have time to watch TV or read a book."

The end of her business day is only the beginning of another job stint as wife and mother. In her few hours between leaving her office and going to bed, dinner needs to be cooked, a two-year-old child cared for, and household chores finished. Her husband, Stephen Baum, helps, and all their jobs do get done.

The Baums freely chose their way of life; they met when they were both students at the Harvard Graduate School of Business Administration. Still, Stephen Baum says, "sometimes we both sit down and look at each other and wonder if it's worth it."

Other couples sometimes wonder the same thing. They are couples who have discarded the premise that a woman's job is her husband's career. Instead, they have chosen a life in which both spouses pursue careers. The Department of Labor knows that there are more than 20 million married women in the work force, but it does not know how many of these are true career women. If the Baums are statistical nonentities, however, their problems and pressures are all too real.

"Nothing in a dual-career marriage can be taken for granted," says Pauline Bart, professor of sociology in psychiatry at the University of Illinois' medical school. "Everything from career opportunities to household responsibilities is subject to negotiation. Who stays home with a sick child? You can't look it up in Doctor Spock."

There being no authority, dual-career couples are thrown on their own resources. If they number among the wealthy stars, like advertising executive Mary Wells Lawrence and her executive husband Harding Lawrence, those resources are formidable indeed. But most dual-career couples are neither rich nor high-powered. Their lives are vulnerable to career pressures and domestic upsets that drain their energy and absorb their time. Some of their marriages crumble. Others thrive, apparently toughened by the pressures.

"The woman at home and the husband at the office are living two different lives," says Sonia Pressman Fuentes, senior attorney at General Telephone and Electronics Corporation in Stamford, Connecticut. She is happily married to a project officer for the Department of Commerce. "We're living more the same kind of life, and we're closer for it," she says.

For attorney Kristin Glen of New York, however, the tension created by dual careers grew intolerable. Her marriage to another lawyer collapsed. "We both needed time and some loving care to decompress from the office," she says. "There just wasn't enough room for adjustments."

Without children, those adjustments often are easier to make. Until they raise a family, dual-career couples have time and money to lavish on themselves. With two incomes, they can afford to unwind on dream vacations and frequent nights on the town. The arrival of a child changes all that. Suddenly, two incomes must stretch to cover nursemaid and baby-sitting expenses as well as ordinary child-care costs. Time for oneself becomes rare.

"The worst time of day is when I come home and I'm tired and the kids are tired," says Jo Dare Mitchell, a vice president of First National City Bank in New York. "I really miss going home, having a drink, and staring at the walls."

Even without children, the time of dual-career couples is hardly all their own. They are vulnerable to the conflicting demands of separate supervisors. A transfer offered to one or the other of the couple automatically creates a difficulty. Many handle transfer agonies by simply declaring their immovability. "Note: My wife's career is established in this area, so I am not at liberty to relocate," a $40,000-a-year man wrote on his résumé to a New York management placement concern.

An oil company executive chose a road to the top that normally would require time in various field locations. But a few years ago he demanded from the company another route up the ladder because his wife's career was well established in New York. He got what he wanted, but he and his wife worry that an executive with field experience may vault over him the next time a higher job opens up. "In the long run, he may have hurt himself," his wife concedes. "We don't know yet."

When one member of a couple does transfer, the other sometimes resists moving until a suitable job appears. Janet Jones, an executive director of a Manhattan firm that recruits women executives, tells about a couple who both held good jobs in Europe. The husband's promotion sent him to New York. His wife kept her job in Europe for more than six months while she sought a New York job that would not mean a downward career step.

Mobile or not, dual-career couples must cope with domestic stresses. Although most divide child care and household duties not handled by hired help, women typically assume a greater share. "Most women try to do everything in the house plus everything expected of them at work," says Professor Bart of Illinois. "This is practical only if you don't need much sleep." A harried career woman says, "I feel I even have to sleep fast."

Jo Mitchell of Citibank frequently handles job-related work at home between four and six o'clock in the morning and then makes breakfast for her two sons and her husband. "Being a wife and a mother is something expected of you," she says. "I work because I need the gratification of doing a job well." Under pressure to do all her duties well, resentment and temper flare. When she and her husband, Robert, both have had a hard day at the office, she sometimes finds herself scurrying to prepare dinner and help the children with their pajamas while Robert is reading the newspaper. He hears about it. "There are always some creature habits that are hard to break," says Robert Mitchell, a computer consultant. "I didn't use to do household chores, so my performance isn't uniform."

Other women smother their resentment, sometimes because they feel guilty for not handling the house as well as they think they should. "Resentment and guilt make a funny stew," says Susanne Schad-Somers, a New York psychotherapist who has many career women as patients. "Responses alternate between migraine headaches, back pains, and doing Sunday dinner extra well."

Even so, most career wives are far from trading the satisfaction and fulfillment of their professional work for a less pressured life. Sharon Baum of Chemical Bank still replays in her mind a period in which she was put to the test, though. At the time, her baby cried every morning when she went to work. "I would hear his sobs—'Mommy come back!'—while I was waiting for the elevator," she recalls with a shudder. After what seemed like hours, the elevator would come to rescue her from the pitiful cries. "I had to keep telling myself I'd feel worse cooped up with him all day," Baum says.

Because their main role has always been the breadwinner's, professional men suffer none of that kind of anxiety or guilt. Nonetheless, husbands in dual-career marriages do encounter hardships. For one thing, although many companies have relaxed rules against employing a husband and wife, most companies ignore the dual-career couple's special problems. And this falls as hard on husbands as on wives in matters like transfers and entertaining clients. "Corporations don't go out of their way to accommodate working couples," says Frank Manley, a management consultant whose wife also pursues a career. Many executives may be simply unaware of the difficulties. Most husbands and wives avoid working out domestic problems in the office out of fear that they will be considered weak links in the chain. "You can't go to the company with your problems," an executive says. "The more you bring it into the office, the more people can use it against you."

"If you've got a problem with your wife, your boss may be sympathetic," a New York husband whose wife works alongside him says, "but not if he's her boss too."

At work, the colleagues of a dual-career husband often have the ready—and visible—mobility that appears when both husband and housewife are united to promote his career alone. At home, the husband of a housewife may unwind with a waiting martini. Dual-career husbands often must play by a different set of rules, one of which is to mix your own martini. When writer Warren Farrell's wife, an IBM executive, cooked him homemade soup recently because he had a cold, tears welled in his eyes. "It was that feeling of being cared for," he says. "Neither one of us has much time for these little supportive things."

Dual-career husbands miss other things. Often there is no one at home to telephone and say, "Honey, pack my bags. I'm off to Chicago." Neither can such husbands ever assume that their wives will be willing or able to entertain clients or attend company gatherings.

In a pinch, the husband and wife may rush to each other's aid, however. Sharon Baum had three business meetings and a desk load of work one recent snowy afternoon. At 12:45, her son's nursery school called to say his nurse had failed to fetch him. Baum telephoned her husband at work, and he took the afternoon off to sit with the child at the couple's apartment. "The most important ingredient in a dual-career marriage," she says wryly, "is a reliable nurse."

7

The "Male Pill"

The time: the early 1980s. The place: the office of an andrologist, a specialist in disorders of the male reproductive system. A young patient comes in to ask about birth control. "Well," the doctor tells him, "you can take your choice of the male pill, ultrasonic treatments, or a reversible vasectomy."

The scenario is less farfetched than it sounds. For the first time since an Italian anatomist invented the condom in 1564, scientists foresee the development of at least one new male contraceptive, possibly within the next five to eight years. Ideally, it would cause temporary sterility without impairing a man's sex drive, his sexual characteristics, or his general health. The researchers' optimism, however guarded, springs from a series of promising new discoveries about the complex male reproductive system. Scientists are exploring new ways to interfere with the production, maturation, or transportation of the average of 80 million sperm contained in every ejaculation of semen. "There's a tremendous amount of work blossoming," says Dr. Philip Corfman, director of the federal Center for Population Research in Bethesda, Maryland. "We feel there's a great need for a modern male method of contraception."

Clearly, male contraception is an idea whose time has come. Long relegated to the back burners of scientific inquiry, it has become a hot topic in laboratories around the land. In fiscal 1974, federal funds for male fertility projects exceeded those awarded for female fertility studies for the first time. Andrology has emerged as a new medical specialty. It is concerned with male fertility in much the same way that gynecology has dealt with the female reproductive system.

"Historically, there have been few people working on male reproduction," says Gabriel Bialy, chief of the Population Research Center's contraceptive development branch. "That's changing. It's not fifty-fifty yet, but it's climbing steadily." Spurring the scientific shift is a growing concern over population growth, coupled with fears that long use of birth-control pills or intrauterine devices (IUDs) may be harmful to some women. Family planning experts suggest that the potential hazards of these birth-control methods might be lessened if a wider variety of contraceptive methods were available to allow a man and a woman to alternate contraception. Many fertility researchers also are persuaded that perfection of a male contraceptive may occur sooner than discovery of a safer substitute for the female pill.

Traditionally, pregnancy and the prevention of pregnancy have been treated as a woman's problem. Feminists contend that the attitude is shared by many doctors and helps explain why so little scientific work, until recently, has gone into male contraception. Most of the 35 million married Americans practicing birth control use methods or materials such as the pill, the IUD, and the diaphragm, which are designed for women. Most couples reject the condom as unreliable and awkward. Only 16 percent considered it the preferred method of contraception, according to a 1970 government survey.

Now, however, men appear to be rethinking their role in contraception. Vasectomy, the male sterilization procedure, is gaining in popularity. Some 4 million American men have chosen to limit family size by vasectomy. To family-planning experts, this suggests that even more would be willing to assume the responsibility for contraception if they could do so without a surgical procedure. Donald Bogue, a sociologist who directs the University of Chicago's Family Study Center, says that surveys in the United States and abroad show that "if there were a male contraceptive that was no more inconvenient than the female pill, and the threat to health were no greater, men would share the burden equally with women." There is other evidence of that. Several researchers in the field of male contraceptives report that even before beginning clinical studies they have received a flood of letters from men asking to try an experimental drug or treatment because, for health reasons, their wives cannot use the pill or the IUD.

Despite some progress, development of a male antifertility agent has unfolded slowly. One hurdle is the increased possibility of genetic damage and birth defects arising from employment of a male contraceptive. Hormones that reduce sperm output could harm the genes carried by a few surviving sperm. If against all odds one of these sperm managed to penetrate a female egg, the result could be a seriously abnormal fetus.

Some drug companies, too, burdened by federal testing requirements and lawsuits over the adverse effects of the pill and the IUD, have cut back on contraceptive research. While the federal government and nonprofit research groups have more than taken up the slack, the $20 million a year they spend falls far short of the $100 million a year that the Ford Foundation estimates it would cost to develop a successful contraceptive in the shortest possible time.

The fruits of the research undertaken so far suggest that a chemical approach to male birth control is the most promising. Limited trials of synthetic male and female sex hormones have been taking place in ten nations. There is intense research interest in a male contraceptive that would combine synthetic testosterone, a hormone that regulates sperm output, with an analog called danazol. An analog has a molecular structure similar to the substance to which it is analogous, but its chemical composition differs a bit. Beginning in 1973, University of Washington School of Medicine researchers gave ninety-five young men daily danazol tablets and monthly testosterone injections for five to six months. At the most effective dosage, sperm disappeared or dropped to very low levels in 85 percent of the subjects. Sperm counts returned to normal three to five months after the treatments ended. Other than a slight gain in weight, the volunteers showed no side effects, says Dr. C. Alvin Paulsen, the medical professor who headed the study. In further trials, Dr. Paulsen hopes to perfect the effectiveness of the method and determine whether lower danazol dosages could work as well. He furthermore hopes to allay fears that the contraceptive could prove to be potentially as hazardous as the female pill, which also combines two sex hormones. Oral contraceptives have been linked to an increased risk of blood clots and high blood pressure. The testosterone-danazol combination "isn't any safer," asserts Dr. Bruce Pharris, principal scientist at Alza Corporation, which is actively involved in contraceptive research. "In fact," he says, "it's got some unknowns that we didn't have in the female pill."

In 1975, the Center for Population Research began a two-year clinical trial of synthetic testosterone in some 100 subjects. Preliminary study has shown that when testosterone builds up sufficiently in the bloodstream, sperm production ceases. Both testosterone and progestin, the female sex hormone, pose safety problems. Testosterone causes a rise in blood fats in certain men. That could increase the risk of heart disease. Among the several hundred men who have taken progestin as a contraceptive, a few have reported breast swelling and decreased sex drive.

If chemical approaches seem most promising, even with their hazards, nonchemical means of male birth control are still being examined. The reversible vasectomy is one of them. The ordinary procedure involves cutting and tying the two vas deferens, the tubes through which sperm travel from the testicles to the urinary tract. To make the procedure reversible, researchers can surgically implant a half-inch-long valve in one of the tubes. When the blocked tube is reopened, the sperm are free to reach the urinary tract once more.

The valves, or "sperm switches," are being developed at about ten American universities and private laboratories. Scientists at the Illinois Institute of Technology's Research Institute in Chicago have found that flexible silicone valves can

turn sperm flow on and off in 90 percent of the experimental
dogs in their study. When the device is reopened, the dogs can
impregnate females even though their sperm count is only
one-fourth the preimplantation level.

Yet human trials have been less successful. Bionyx Corporation, of Bohemia, New York, implanted its gold valve, trade
named the Phaser, in 100 men who had sought vasectomies.
The devices later were removed from half the subjects. Their
sperm would not flow through the sperm tube when the valve
was reopened. Further studies have shown this to be a consequence of trauma from the insertion procedure. After the valve
remains in place for a year, however, such problems appear to
vanish. "I'm convinced we're on the right track," says Louis
Bucalo, Bionyx president. "I think we'll have a device soon
that we can market as a contraceptive." But Dr. Joseph E.
Davis, professor of urology at New York Medical College and a
consultant to Bionyx, is more cautious. "It will take a few more
years before it is commercially available," he says of the
Phaser.

Ultrasonics could provide a method of male birth control.
Animals become temporarily infertile when their testes are
treated with low levels of silent, high-frequency vibrations,
often used in physical therapy as a heat source. Mostafa S.
Fahim, professor and chief of reproductive biology at the University of Missouri School of Medicine, discovered ultrasound's effectiveness while exploring the contraceptive potential of heat. Hot baths, steam, a fever, or tight-fitting pants
long have been known to reduce male fertility.

Still, Professor Fahim believes that the vibrations of ultrasound, not its heat, curb sperm output. He theorizes that
ultrasonic waves alter the molecular composition of certain
chemicals in testicular cells so that sperm manufacture is dis-
rupted. After two years of rat studies, he decided that ultrasound does not affect sexual behavior and causes no
short-term side effects. Two treatments in one week appear
sufficient to impair fertility for one year in rats, dogs, cats,
goats, and monkeys. Definitive studies on human beings
are in progress. "It will take a lot of time and research,"
Professor Fahim concedes. He eventually must show that

prolonged exposure to ultrasound will not affect the sperm's genetic makeup, cause permanent sterility, or otherwise damage the reproductive system.

Professor Fahim has designed a chair apparatus for administering ultrasound to patients in doctors' offices. Someday, he believes, an ultrasonic contraceptive machine may be found in the ordinary household bathroom.

8

More for Fewer

The future of education now seems a bit different from the one most educators predicted in 1966. They correctly foresaw major trends: increasing demand for adult education, new flexibility in the content and structure of education, a great expansion in corporate education training. The experts perceived the impact of computers and other electronics advances. But they did not estimate correctly the time it would take to get new technology into widespread use.

They went wrong in other ways, too. They thought the outpouring of government and foundation money into education would never stop growing. They conceived of education as the new growth industry. They expected school enrollments to continue soaring at all levels. And they worried about how to manage the staggering amount of new construction all this would require.

Over the past twenty-five years, the age group of ten- to thirty-year-olds has whirled the normally change-resistant education field through boom and bust. Today, the generation born between 1946 and 1967 forms a bulging aberration on the population charts, a group that will comprise one-third of the citizenry for the rest of the century. The births of the people in

45

this group touched off education's boom. Their unexpected decision to breed fewer babies than their parents helped bring about a bust—sort of.

"I shudder at how cloudy was that crystal ball," says Harold B. Gores, president of Educational Facilities Laboratories, Inc., a nonprofit research concern. Besides the unexpected drop in the birthrate, he says, "what we all failed to observe was that we were about to pass out of the era of cheap labor, cheap energy, and cheap money. No one seemed to foresee that education and economics were on a collision course."

"Higher education's prospects resemble the perils of Pauline," says Paul C. Reinert, chancellor of St. Louis University.

The total school-age population (five years of age to twenty-four) once was expected to swell to 125 million by 2000. Instead, it now is expected to number only 79 million, plus, perhaps, another 6 million early-starting three- and four-year-olds, up only 1 million from 78 million today.

During the past generation, salaries, construction, and other expenditures on formal education grew from a little over 2 percent of the gross national product to 8 percent. Only one other major sector of the economy, the military, increased its spending at such a rate. Now, the most generous forecasts put education spending at 12 percent of GNP by 2000, against earlier forecasts of 25 percent.

Of the money to be spent on education, greater shares than in the past are expected to go to increase "productivity." Computer and other electronic teaching systems will be more widely used. Emptying school and college buildings will be converted into adult learning centers. Promoting adult demand for education, many educators believe, offers one way of offsetting the relative decline in the school-age population.

Few new school facilities will arise during the rest of the century. Most of them will be relatively low-cost glass fiber structures with lives of twenty years. They are expected to house recreational facilities shared with municipal recreation departments, company employee athletic programs, and perhaps even private health clubs. Brick-and-mortar construction will go to convert unused campus dormitories into apartments for married students, faculty, and retirees, and to renovate empty elementary schools for public or private use.

Already the percentage of high school students going on to college has slipped from a peak of 55 percent in 1968 to about 47 percent. Rising tuitions, the end of the draft, and bleaker job prospects have discouraged enrollments. Experts once thought that 85 percent of high school graduates would go to college by 1990. They now expect 50 percent at most. This means that colleges may be educating only 13.2 million students in 2000 instead of the 17 million to 22 million once anticipated. But by then, lifelong education and training may be the norm. Many Americans will enter school at age three and get the equivalent of two years of college; throughout their lives, they will drop in and out of the educational system to update their job skills, study for new careers, or delve into art, music, literature, or languages for the fun of it.

"Learning centers" akin to today's language schools and art workshops will be established in offices, factories, storefronts, and public buildings. Computers and videodiscs, nearly as accessible as books are today, will bring study into the home. More generous sabbaticals and employer-paid tuition plans will be widespread. Or so many educators expect.

The shape of things to come can already be discerned in some places. The University of Mid-America, a joint venture of five state universities in the Midwest, now uses traveling faculty and educational television to teach adults who cannot attend classes on campus. At eleven company offices and two industrial parks in Los Angeles, desk-top television sets and intercoms provide instruction from the University of Southern California's school of engineering. "Weekend college" programs for adults have sprung up around the country.

These trends toward decentralization and diversity are a far cry from what many educators foresaw ten years ago. Even in primary and secondary education, consolidation is slowing. And educational planners expect continued growth in smaller, scattered, specialized public schools, each stressing a particular discipline, whether languages, mathematics, music, or carpentry, that will draw pupils from miles around.

Many experts believe also that some kind of voucher system, now being tested in California and New Hampshire, will help finance education. Checklike vouchers would be issued to taxpayers and parents to "buy" education in schools of their choice. Inferior schools, or so the theory goes, would be forced to improve or close for lack of students. A voucher system might promote a great deal of classroom integration, not only racial. Precocious ten-year-olds would be free to take courses with teenagers and middle-aged homemakers, retired people, and even mentally and physically handicapped youngsters now considered "uneducable" in many schools.

Formal classroom education overseen by professional teachers will provide just a part of instruction in the future. A California experiment may take hold elsewhere. In 1975, 43,000 parents and 37,000 student volunteers trooped into California schools to help teach to first, second, and third graders such skills as grammar and carpentry. Meanwhile, 600 high school juniors and seniors went outside their schools to learn such things as drafting and secretarial work in five Rockwell International Corporation plants in the Los Angeles area.

"By 2000," says Wilson N. Riles, California's state superintendent of public instruction, "it won't be necessary to go to high school every day. There won't be such a thing as a nine-month school. There will be year-round opportunities for learning, and the whole community will be the classroom."

Property taxes, a portion of which will be allocated statewide to equalize school budgets, will remain the most important source of educational financing. But federal money will continue to become more important, perhaps by 2000 paying one-third, up from 10 percent currently, of all elementary, secondary, and higher education costs.

Some educators expect the federal Office of Education to evolve into a full-fledged regulatory agency. "By 2000, the state and federal governments will tell us whom we can hire and fire," says Ralph K. Huitt, executive director of the National Association of State Universities and Land-Grant Colleges.

The phenomenal growth of community colleges already may have peaked. They had been expected to enroll 6 million students by 2000, up from only 850,000 in 1965 and 4.1 million in 1976. "It will be 6 million [in 2000] if you include courses like flower arranging, juggling, and fly tying, but that's essentially tax-supported entertainment," says Arthur M. Cohen, a professor of higher education at UCLA whose specialty is community colleges.

Some private colleges will have disappeared by 2000. And research-oriented institutions like the University of Chicago, Harvard and Yale Universities, University of Michigan, University of California at Berkeley, and MIT will compete fiercely for a shrinking pool of research grants. State colleges and universities will stress job training, but not through conventional vocational courses.

"There will be more of a connection between what you're studying and the vocation toward which you're pointing, but with it will be renewed interest in liberal arts," says Ernest L. Boyer, chancellor of the State University of New York. "There'll be a sharpening of the view that being an educated person has something to do with goodness and values. We're going to have to prepare better for the ethical and moral issues that grow out of our expected vocations."

Earl Pullias, professor of higher education at the University of Southern California, agrees. "It's not enough to produce just knowledgeable or highly trained people," he says. "The American people are concerned with the deterioration of integrity. Higher education has abdicated in this area, even though one of its original purposes was to further develop values. We must regrasp that role."

Today, some educators think, even highly educated Americans are confused by advanced technology and cannot be expected to explore the ethical implications of progress until they understand its technical underpinnings. "Years ago," says Joseph L. Shapiro, a futurist at Gillette Company, "a doctor of philosophy was a sort of Renaissance man. Now he's a very narrow specialist. Outside of his own little splinter of expertise, he doesn't feel like he has much of a handle on anything going on around him. And neither does anybody else."

Television may provide the "handle." More of prime-time commercial TV, State University of New York's Boyer thinks, "will be devoted to general education. We are increasingly going to have to talk to ourselves about emerging patterns and trends in everything from hunger to international terrorism.

Prime-time TV is going to provide what are, in effect, seminars to educate us on those concerns."

Universities and private educational concerns are expected to increase their output of video recordings exploring public issues. Through such recordings, obscure professors may become national celebrities. Home viewers may have easy access to video documentaries ranging from the aesthetically ascetic to the hard-core pornographic, in either case complete with stop-action and instant replay.

Video-packaged education is expected to encourage the elimination of formal course and time requirements to earn high school diplomas and college degrees. But standardized tests will be back in vogue to determine whether students have mastered their subjects.

Most educated Americans will have some expertise in computers. Even now, at Spence School, a private girls' school in New York, second graders are being taught to use the school's sixteen computer terminals for mathematics drills. Students in Spence's high school courses use the computer in such disciplines as biochemistry and nuclear physics. "It works sensationally well in developing both computational skills and real understanding of rarefied mathematics," says Dustin H. Heuston, headmaster.

As every owner of a portable calculator knows, miniaturization and other advances in computer technology and production have greatly reduced costs. Three years ago, Heuston observes, Spence paid $12,400 for the minicomputer the school now employs. "Today," he says, "I could buy the same capacity for about $5,000, and in a few more years it will cost under $1,000."

Relatively inexpensive computer programs will permit the study of obscure subjects at low cost. At Stanford University, a computer already teaches a course in Old Church Russian. "It's too expensive to hire an instructor for such a small course," says Patrick Suppes, director of the university's institute for mathematical studies in the social sciences. Suppes oversees an introductory logic course, taught entirely by computer, for 180 Stanford students.

Summary

From the foregoing pictures of America in the future, a vision emerges. Trends that now are clearly visible produce not a typical American family or consumer but an array of highly individualized groups, subcultures, and specimens. Already, as the profile of Gillette Company's Joseph L. Shapiro shows, forward-thinking management is sifting ideas for exploiting this changing consumer market.

Values are undergoing a radical transformation. A large proportion of half the nation's population, its women, seems likely to become disenchanted at anything less than the prospect of "meaningful" work and careers. The stigma of divorce, dissipating for the past generation, has disappeared in all but the most traditional-minded American communities. Single people have emerged as respectable and responsible members of society. Homosexuals are winning judicial recognition of their civil rights.

For various reasons, too, each member of these disparate groups is achieving greater economic freedom. That means that members of the "new minorities" will continue to increase their influence in the marketplace. Put more bluntly, the single person, the woman, or the homosexual of the future will have more money and will find himself or herself with the power to command the attention and respect of corporations.

Bankers in Des Moines or Tucson still may blanch at the idea, but any New York banker unwilling to lend mortgage money to "living together" singles may well find himself excluded from some of the city's prime housing markets even today. It is not difficult to believe that twenty-five years from now, bankers generally will ignore such factors as the marital status or sexual preferences of their loan applicants. This is all the easier to appreciate when we keep in mind that the consumer loans aggressively solicited by bankers today would have been deemed risk-laden and frivolous by most bankers twenty-five years ago.

Managers at many corporations already have had to adjust to changes brought about by the employment of women in larger numbers and in more desirable, highly-paid jobs. Provisions for rest rooms and child-care centers are obvious responses; changes in pension funding to accommodate the longer life expectancies of women are less obvious but at least as important to the corporate financial officer. The problems that beset the company personnel manager, dealing with such matters as sick leave for pregnancy, maternity benefits, and other questions arising from female employment, are likely to increase in the future.

On the marketing side, corporate management will have to cope with subtler questions in the future. For many years, manufacturers and marketers of consumer products have found in their "mix" a strategy for maximizing profits. Careful calculations balancing price, quality, and taste have enabled the maker and marketer of consumer goods to provide an array of products that sell to dealers and to individual consumers at a profit.

This strategy has created such products as the television and FM-stereo console housed in the Renaissance cabinet, a quintessential acquisition in suburbia. Yet the suburbia envisioned by this kind of strategy no longer exists, its male breadwinners seemingly being preoccupied with the design of their own sound systems or with citizens'-band radio or even with turning carpenters.

Among America's huge corporations, J. C. Penney and others have had the foresight and good fortune to anticipate some striking changes in consumer behavior and demand. There is still no indication, however, that the upsurge of individualism in taste and demand has reached a peak. The nation's sophisticated marketing managements are more carefully gearing their products and services to specific age groups. The "life cycle" has become a subject of serious study. A Des Moines insurance company offers a "life cycle" policy with premiums increasing and decreasing in proportion to changes in the policyholder's income and insurance-protection needs. In 1976, the U.S. Department of Housing and Urban Development began insuring home loans under a graduated mortgage payment plan. Aimed at young home-owners, the plan reduces payments in the early years of a mortgage loan below standard levels. Later, monthly payments rise above standard levels—at a time when the no-longer-quite-so-young couple has enjoyed an increase in income and spending power. And computerized consumer data available from mailing lists and credit-information banks have enabled practically all of American business to identify and reach highly individualized groups of potential customers.

Corporate planners are likely to rely increasingly on social and behavioral research to perceive at least the dim outlines of future markets. In retrospect, as some of the foregoing chapters show, the striking changes in America's consumer markets were predictable. So are changes in the consumer markets of the future.

II
SURVIVAL
Health and Food

9

The United States and World Hunger

It is late September 2000. Another subfreezing morning, the Secretary of Food Policy notes as he boards an Ottawa-bound flight at Washington with his subordinates, the Secretary of Agriculture and the Secretary of State. Again, the monsoon rains have failed in Asia. The American corn harvest looks good by year-2000 standards. But why, the Secretary asks himself, can't somebody develop a 90-day corn that would yield the way 120-day corn did back in the 1970s? If it weren't for frosts nearly every May and September, he muses, the high-yielding long-season corn would still mature. And wouldn't it be nice to pile on the chemical fertilizer?

In Ottawa, the entourage is met by its Canadian counterparts. After perfunctory greetings, the delegations get down to the grim yearly task before them: rationing the food produced by their nations to the rest of the world.

If all this seems improbable, it is not nearly so unlikely as it might have seemed in 1966. Today, the United States and Canada produce about 80 percent of all the world's export grain. By 2000, some agricultural experts say, they may be the only two countries in the world that produce more grain than they consume. And they may well decide, in the fashion of the

57

Organization of Petroleum Exporting Countries, who gets how much and at what price. Grain is the key foodstuff. Directly or indirectly (after being consumed by animals) it accounts for 70 percent of what the world eats.

In 1966, world hunger was discussed only by the most foresighted, and largely in us-against-them terms. But it will touch the lives of Americans. It may create a major change in the American diet and in the structure of American agriculture. Food may be the most powerful force in international politics and domestic economics, and the "food issue" may be the leading one in the presidential election of 2000.

Two developments since 1966 have affected all projections about food. One is the energy crisis. The other is the weather. In 1966, experts and seers implicitly assumed that cheap energy and favorable weather were here to stay.

It now appears that they were not.

There was a major nondevelopment, too. Though Americans have done their share, the world as a whole has made little progress in reducing the rate of population growth. By 2000, the present world population of 3.9 billion will have grown to nearly 7 billion. Before 2050, it will double to 14 billion.

That means, according to studies by the United Nations and others, that food production will have to grow by an average of 3.6 percent to 4 percent a year if all those people are to be fed. These growth rates are impossibly high, many analysts believe. They say the world will be hard pressed to match its recent food-growth rate of less than 3 percent a year, a rate that still leaves anywhere from 500 million to 1.5 billion people underfed.

The high cost of petroleum threatens the efficiency of America as a food-producing machine. David Pimentel, a food scientist at Cornell University, estimates that the 240 percent increase in American corn yields between 1946 and 1970 was accompanied by a 310 percent increase in the energy used to produce that corn.

That increase was at the farming level. Other links in the food production chain, from the tractor factory to the food processor to the supermarket, consume perhaps four times as much energy as the nation's farms. John Steinhart, food and energy analyst at the University of Wisconsin, says that the American food system now uses about ten calories of fuel for every calorie of food consumed. Higher fuel costs, then, at the very least, mean higher food prices, and one study suggests that a tripling of fuel costs ultimately doubles food prices.

At some point, too, no increase in the price of food will increase its supply. "Modern agriculture . . . is an energy consumer of a magnitude that raises profound doubts as to its ability . . . to prevent wholesale starvation," a special report on food by the National Science Foundation said in 1975.

Most spectacularly in India, but also in other parts of the world, the heralded "green revolution" in farm productivity appears to have ground to a halt or slowed considerably because of the high cost and scarcity of energy.

At the same time, the weather has taken a sharp turn for the worse, perhaps as part of a long-term cycle. Some weather experts believe that the American farm belt is in the early stage of a long drought. Some think temperatures in the northern temperate zones are cooling, and that the trend will produce frequent frosts and shorter growing seasons. And some suspect that monsoon rain failures in Asia are increasing. Only one such failure occurred in the 1960s. So far in the 1970s, there have been two.

Even if the current weather is "normal," experts say, Mother Nature was unusually bountiful during the 1960s, when there were no major weather-caused crop failures anywhere in the world. Weather historians quote the odds against such a decade at 10,000 to 1. "Each good year now just increases the probability of bad ones in the future," a weather researcher says.

It is a statement of fact, rather than a prediction, to say that food is going to cost substantially more in the year 2000. As recently as 1966, food prices in the United States were rising less than 3 percent a year, and the *Wall Street Journal* was able to talk of "quite possibly cheaper" food in 2000. Now food economists think that the family spending $50 a week for food today may be spending $150 a week (in today's dollars) in the year 2000.

Americans will eat less food, probably, and certainly less of some kinds of food. Marbled grain-fed beef, a mainstay of many diets for generations, apparently is becoming a luxury. The steer is an inefficient converter of grain to meat, and Kenneth Monfort, cochairman of Monfort of Colorado, Inc., the country's largest feedlot operator, says beef consumption "will drop dramatically."

Economics aside, some voices are challenging the desirability of pouring more grain into beef when human beings elsewhere in the world have too little grain. Many people in the meat industry dispute the assumptions underlying this view, but the sentiment still appears to be growing. "The amount of grain put into animal production in this country is a national disgrace," says Georg Borgstrom, a food scientist at Michigan State University. "We've had this enormous banquet at a time when the world was rapidly moving to the edge of the precipice."

None of this means an end to the beef business. "It certainly will mean a significant shift in the way we manage the beef animal," says Robert Bray, animal scientist at the University of Wisconsin. In the early 1970s, grain became so expensive that many cattle were turned out to graze the open range, just as they did in pioneering days, when grain was dear. Grazing animals accounted for about half of all beef produced in the United States in 1975, and they may account for as much as 90 percent, some analysts believe, by 2000.

The steer's relative efficiency in converting grass, corn stalks, and other cheap forage into beef assures the critter's survival. But today, some analysts say, there is insufficient forage land to support the cattle population, and there will be even less in 2000, so total beef output will fall.

The hog may have a bleaker future because it is no grazing ruminant, and the pork chop might become a greater luxury than the steak in 2000. "I fear what might happen to pork production in this country," Bray says.

To some people it is a disturbing paradox that the Soviet Union and Japan, along with rich oil-exporting countries, are trying to consume more meat. Russia's big grain purchases in recent years went not to make bread to stave off hunger, but to increase livestock feeding and produce, inefficiently, more meat protein.

Research in meat substitutes will become more urgent. "If we can develop a palatable substitute for meat," says Jean Mayer, formerly professor of nutrition at Harvard who was named president of Tufts University in 1976, "we'll have made a great advance in the fight against hunger." Soybean-based meat analogs are on the market, though some people think their taste leaves a bit to be desired. At the moment, the question is academic because analogs cost more than the real thing. As the year 2000 nears and analogs become relatively cheap, some analysts think that perhaps half the "fresh meat" in a typical supermarket will consist of soybean, wheat gluten, or some other nonmeat protein.

Ten years ago, food experts talked of "methodically harvesting the oceans" for a big part of the food supply in 2000. That prospect has dimmed because of pollution, overfishing, and international squabbling over fishing rights. After rising steadily from 1950 to 1970, the world fish catch fell in three of the five years since 1970, and some people believe the ocean already is contributing as much as it ever will to the food supply.

Much research is directed toward developing look-alike, taste-alike substitutes for today's conventional foods, because even in underfed nations, resistance to dietary changes is strong. "The bulk of our effort is to make sure the product doesn't change much," says John Luck, technical director at General Mills, Inc. "I don't believe that in the year 2000 we'll be living on exotic foods" such as krill, algae, or single-cell organisms.

A few surprises could be in store. "What's difficult to estimate is the impact of triticale [a wheat-rye cross] and other results of genetic manipulation," Mayer says. "We may have a food supply quite different from today's."

To maintain or increase yields of crops people already eat, researchers are spending a lot of time studying photosynthesis. This is the intriguing, awesome, but inefficient process by which plants use light to turn carbon dioxide and water into carbohydrates. All food ultimately derives from the process.

To make photosynthesis more productive, researchers are trying such things as breeding plants with more leaf surface exposed to light and trapping higher levels of carbon dioxide in man-made environments.

All plants require nitrogen. Most of them fail to get enough to realize their growth potential without large quantities of nitrogen fertilizer. Some plants, however, especially legumes like alfalfa and soybeans, obtain nitrogen from the air through the work of nitrogen-fixing bacteria. Scientists speculate that they can breed bacteria to do the same thing for other plants, like corn. Success would constitute a major breakthrough. "Theoretically," a researcher says, "you could take these bacteria, throw them on a field of corn and fertilize it—and win fifteen Nobel Prizes all at once."

But that is all theoretical and speculative. "For the immediate future," concludes a report on agriculture by the National Academy of Sciences, "there will be continued advances in technology for both plants and livestock, but no startling breakthroughs that could place production on a new level."

So sober a view would have been heretical ten years ago, when the *Wall Street Journal* concluded that "in the not too distant future" it might be possible "to produce close to 500 bushels of corn an acre." The average in 1975 in Illinois, the top corn-producing state, was 116 bushels. "There is increasing evidence that yields are plateauing," says Glenn Pound, dean of the college of agriculture at the University of Wisconsin. "There is no way we can expect yields to continue to increase in the next thirty-five years as they have in the past thirty-five." Moreover, he and others observe, there is insufficient additional acreage to counteract a stagnation in yield.

Future farmers will work their land somewhat differently. They will not manage their fields from "towers containing television scanners to keep an eye on robot tractors," as one observer expected ten years ago. "That's an exciting thing to draw pictures of, but it costs too much," says R. E. Baumheckel, production research manager at International Harvester Company. But Baumheckel does foresee "larger and far more sophisticated" farm machines, and in his opinion, almost every farmer will use borrowed computer time to plan planting, purchases of capital equipment, and other strategic activities.

At the same time, other experts believe that a worsening of the energy crisis might return older farming technology and production arrangements to favor. Farmers might, for example, use less chemical fertilizer and pesticide, more animal manure and natural pest killers. They might resume crop rotation to preserve soil nutrients. Farmers might buy smaller, less energy-consuming gear, and farms might become smaller. With energy a scarce commodity, bigness would not necessarily create economies of scale.

Agriculture might become more labor-intensive, and some people even see a return to draft animals for certain farm work. Steinhart, at the University of Wisconsin, thinks home gardening and even subsistence farming will make "not insignificant contributions to future food supplies."

The waste of food almost certainly will disappear, most experts say, and food generally will be more carefully considered in terms of health and nutrition. Authoritative "food efficacy committees" may pass on the merits of foods, Howard Bauman, vice president of science and technology for Pillsbury Company, thinks. New professions may combine medicine and food science. Some day, Bauman says, it will be possible to perform biochemical tests on a newborn child that will "determine what his diet should be throughout his life." For some people, that is an Orwellian prospect. Paul Khan, director of food protection at ITT Continental Baking Company, asks, "Is RDA—recommended daily allowance—going to mean required daily allotment?"

But an even greater nightmare is the prospect that North America will be forced to decide who will be and will not be fed in 2000.

North America's 80 percent share of world grain exports represents a striking change. As recently as the 1930s, observes Lester R. Brown, president of Worldwatch Institute, a research group in Washington, D.C., the world outside Western Europe was a net exporter of grain. North America was exporting 5 million tons a year, compared with 96 million tons estimated for fiscal 1976, and even Latin America and Asia exported grain.

Yet the United States already has made selective allocations of foodstuffs. In 1973, it halted soybean shipments to Japan. In 1975, it stopped grain exports to Russia and Poland. "We told these countries, 'No, you can't have any food, at least for the time being,' " Brown says. By 2000, he says, this selective allocation may give way to a "systematic allocation on a country-by-country basis."

Another observer thinks this would require "horrifying, excruciating" decisions that would be greatly complicated by the vagaries of weather. If the monsoons fail repeatedly, and if North America and the Soviet Union suffer major crop failures at the same time, the "gigantic, inevitable famine" that Thomas Malthus predicted in 1798 may become real.

10

The Strange Change in Climate

Sexy locusts in North Africa, sticky wickets in England, and ice fields in the Arctic would seem to have little to do with drought that blisters the lands bordering the southern Sahara and northwest India. But they have a lot to do with it. These and a host of other obvious or obscure clues are coming under the close scrutiny of scientists trying to unravel the mystery of drought—what causes it and how to forecast it. So far the evidence is scant and the conclusions drawn from it are theoretical and speculative. But there are grounds for believing that drought is part of a massive climatic shift that bodes ill for all mankind.

Drought may linger for decades. Drought may invade new areas.

Throughout history, periodic droughts have denied man the sustaining rains for his crops and livestock. On occasion they have been long and severe enough to disrupt and even destroy civilizations. Before man, geological records show, droughts swept large land areas, raising great clouds of dust into the atmosphere and depositing them thousands of miles away. Even today, dust blown from the African drought is blocking a little sunshine in the Caribbean and affecting the weather there.

In the United States, hardly an area has not been hit by drought on occasion. West Texas and South Florida recently have experienced it. Crucial droughts have occurred regularly about every two decades in the Great Plains and the Midwest. The last one was in the mid-1950s. The one before that created the Dust Bowl of the Depression. Proponents of the twenty-year-cycle theory think the country is entering another such drought.

Despite the horrors of the Dust Bowl and other droughts, some evidence suggests that the world may have experienced in the twentieth century one of the most favorable runs of weather ever. But many experts think that weather patterns may be reverting to "normal." For one thing, the earth has gradually cooled over the past three decades. The drop in average temperature is barely perceptible, but it may be enough to cause significant changes in weather.

The implications are staggering. Cooler weather could shorten growing seasons, thereby cutting crop yields in the world's grain belts girdling the United States, Canada, Australia, and Argentina. Under changed weather conditions, crop varieties and farming methods consistent with the weather of the past seventy years might fail to provide the food needed to feed the world's growing population. Small wonder, then, that on land, at sea, and in space, a small army of scientists and researchers are measuring ocean currents and temperatures, tracking changes in the cyclonic winds that sweep eastward around the globe, mapping the shifting polar snow cover, and monitoring hundreds of other variables in the hope of determining whether changes are temporary or long-term.

The first key observations on the current drought were made in 1970 by Derek Winstanley, then affiliated with the Anti-Locust Research Centre in London. In studying the causes of the huge swarming of desert locusts in North Africa the year before, Winstanley found that unusually heavy rains had allowed prolonged breeding by the locusts. Their population exploded.

The heavy rains came from moist air that normally would have dumped water in the northern Mediterranean. Instead, the air was pushed hundreds of miles to the south by prevail-

ing circumpolar currents across Europe, currents that themselves had shifted southward. And that shift forced southward
the hotter and moister airflows called monsoons that boil up
from the equator. The monsoons normally occurred along a
broad line from Mauritania on Africa's west coast across the
Indian Ocean into northwest India. With no monsoons coming, drought struck places along that line.

Air patterns in the northern hemisphere are controlled
largely by great masses of cold air spinning out of the Arctic.
As the earth has cooled over thirty years, the cold air mass
surrounding the North Pole has expanded. So has the snow
and ice covering the Arctic. The cold air masses have broken
into the circumpolar air currents with increasing frequency.

"The shift, in all likelihood, has produced a significant
change in the hemispheric heat balance," conclude George
and Helena Kukla of the Lamont-Doherty Geological Obser-
vatory at Columbia University. They note that the expanding
Arctic ice has exacerbated a heat imbalance. Sunlight absorbed by the earth is the primary source of atmospheric heat.
Vegetation absorbs more than 80 percent of sunlight, oceans
more than 90 percent, but snow and ice absorb only about 20
percent, reflecting the rest back into space without adding to
the atmosphere's heat. This represents a "deficit in the earth's
energy balance," the Kuklas say. In addition, the expanded ice
pack almost completely cuts off atmospheric warming that the
ocean under the pack normally would create.

One primary cause of the shift may be sunspots. Every
eleven years, the number of relatively cool areas on the sun's
surface, appearing as dark spots when viewed through a light
filter, reaches a peak. Then the sun is in its most turbulent
state. Solar storms eject large clouds of particles into space.
Some of them reach earth. J. W. King, a scientist at the Radio
and Space Research Station in England, thinks that these energetic solar particles interact with the earth's atmosphere at
northern latitudes, changing the upper-air pressure and thus
altering weather patterns throughout the hemisphere. Evidence linking sunspots to weather changes is "very strong,"
he says. One study has shown that the growing season in the
north of England between 1916 and 1969 tended to be longest

about one year following the peak of a sunspot cycle. King says that another study shows that the most severe winters in the northeastern United States and north-central Europe corresponded to highs and lows in the sunspot cycle. And a third study, only half-facetious, has shown that English cricket batsmen tended to hit 3,000 runs in a single season—a relatively rare performance—more often in years of sunspot peaks. The wicket (the part of a cricket field on which the ball is thrown and bounced to the batsman) would tend to be wet or sticky during rainy weather; summers of sunspot peaks would tend to have dry, sunny weather, and because fewer games would be canceled during sunny weather, more runs would be scored.

In the United States, some observers think that sunspots are related to the Great Plains drought cycle. But droughts do not occur exactly every twenty-two years; the interval has varied from seventeen years to twenty-five years. There is considerable scientific debate around the world on sunspots and their effects. The link, if any, between sunspots and weather is less than widely accepted.

Another theory has it that more air pollution has contributed to weather changes. Reid A. Bryson, director of the Institute for Environmental Studies at the University of Wisconsin, contends that increased volcanic activity in recent years has put more dust in the air. Dust filters the sun's rays and can account for much of the cooling trend, Bryson thinks. And he says that man has done his part by adding dust from smokestacks and from the slash-and-burn farming practiced in poor lands. Drought in marginal, overfarmed country generates additional dust, he observes.

Fossil-fuel burning throws much carbon dioxide into the atmosphere; its carbon dioxide content has increased by more than 10 percent, some studies estimate, since 1850. This creates some confusion in scientific thinking. Carbon dioxide absorbs heat from the sun, and supposedly that creates a warming, "greenhouse" effect. At one point, in fact, scientists thought that the increased carbon dioxide might eventually heat the earth enough to melt polar ice caps. Instead, the earth has cooled and the ice caps have expanded.

Bryson thinks the heating effect of carbon dioxide has disturbed the temperature gradients between the ground and the upper atmosphere and between the equator and the North Pole, interfering with "normal" air movements. That might help explain the southward shifts, he thinks.

"The evidence is now abundantly clear that the climate of the earth is changing . . . in a direction that is not promising," Bryson told two Senate subcommittees in 1974. He warned that if his analysis is correct, the monsoons on which great areas of the globe depend for survival "probably won't return regularly in this century."

Other respected scientists think Bryson's analysis is incorrect. J. Murray Mitchell, Jr., an expert on climatic variation for the National Oceanic and Atmospheric Administration (NOAA), asserts that natural fluctuations accounted for most of the world's temperature changes in recent decades. Uncontrolled carbon dioxide may become troublesome in the future, he says, but he believes that more active volcanoes, not man, have generated the increased dust that is a key factor in the post-1940s cooling. NOAA scientists estimate that atmospheric dust of all kinds keeps the earth's atmosphere 1.3 degrees centigrade cooler than if there were no such dust. They also estimate that 88.5 percent of the dust is produced by natural processes such as volcanic activity. But they calculate that man-made pollutants may equal natural dust within twenty-three years.

Compared with changes in earlier eras, this century's heating and cooling trends are minor. For the past one million years or longer, great glaciers periodically have swept out from the poles to cover vast areas of the globe. Ice ages have lasted longer than the periods between them. The past two intervals between ice ages lasted for 10,000 years, almost the exact time that has elapsed since the last glaciers covered much of North America, Europe, and Asia.

Does this mean that another ice age is beginning? Nobody knows, but there is speculation. A 1972 conference at Brown University concluded that "the natural end of our present warm epoch is undoubtedly near. . . . Global cooling and related rapid changes in environment substantially exceeding the fluctuations . . . in historic times must be expected within the next few millennia or even centuries."* In the past, scientists at the conference noted, some ice ages have developed in the geologically minuscule span of just a few hundred years. The glaciers are unlikely to start creeping south today or tomorrow. Still, the cooling trend and drought have greatly increased scientific sensitivity to meteorological matters. NOAA has established a small network of widely separated observatories around the world, equipped to detect minute changes in the atmosphere that are thought to be most closely linked with long-term climatic changes. These minute changes occur in solar radiation, atmospheric turbidity, carbon dioxide concentrations, and dozens of other parameters.

Scientists from the Soviet Union and the United States have met to exchange views on climatic changes. American satellites have been monitoring drought areas in Africa. The National Weather Service has supplemented its weekly weather and crop bulletins with charts of drought areas in most of the world's grain-producing lands. World grain stocks have dwindled for several years, reaching their nadir in 1973, as a result of drought and other factors. And world population has reached a point where even in the best weather circumstances it threatens to consume as much grain as could possibly be produced.

That there are any grain reserves at all is owed to a few highly favorable growing seasons in the United States, says research meteorologist James D. McQuigg of the University of Missouri. He observes that American grains need abundant water and long growing seasons for maximum yields. Long-term shifts toward drier, cooler weather would have serious consequences, he says. The National Weather Service's drought charts should provide an early warning of any interruption in grain output, experts think. So far, there is no conclusive evidence that a general American drought has begun. But most authorities think that America's long string of good-weather years must give way, sooner or later, to some extremely poor years.

* G. J. Kukla, R. K. Matthes, and J. M. Mitchell, editors, "The End of the Present Interglacial," *Quaternary Research*, Vol. 2, No. 3, 1972.

11

The Green Revolution

Los Banos, in the Philippines, is a battlefield in the green revolution. The revolutionaries are agronomists, entomologists, microbiologists, agroeconomists, plant breeders, soil chemists, plant physiologists, and geneticists who are pooling their energies and expertise to devise more productive rice plants than nature has produced. The International Rice Research Institute is at Los Banos, and when people mention the green revolution, they are referring to scientific advances made here and at a similar center for wheat research in Mexico. These centers offer at least some hope that the world will be able to provide enough grains to feed mankind.

Unhappily, the key word is merely "hope." There is no assurance that the green revolution will succeed. For every expert prematurely excited over future rice gluts, there is another expert convinced of famine. The scientists at the rice institute are quick to admit that developments that are truly revolutionary in the test tube have proved merely evolutionary, at best, in the rice paddies of the underdeveloped world. Thus the green revolution—or green evolution—still faces many barriers. They range from strong insects to weak politicians, from God's floods to man's ignorance.

71

The latter may prove the more disastrous. The world's population stands at nearly 4 billion and it could double by 2010. The population is growing fastest in the poor nations, where rice is the staple foodstuff. Unless these lands can limit their population growth, food output cannot keep pace. Yet it seems that men with empty bellies have minds empty of plans for the future. It is a vicious quandary which the green revolution has a chance, but only a chance, of ending.

"We have the potential," says Vernon Ross, a rice production expert at the institute, "but if we miss the chance in the next five years, food supply never again may meet demand."

With respect to rice, the green revolution amounts to the development, beginning in the early 1960s, of short-stemmed, stiff-strawed, hybrid varieties that, unlike traditional rices, produce strikingly high yields when chemically fertilized. Some hybrids have genealogies as long and complex as those of contemporary Bourbon princes. The newest of the bunch offer a fair degree of genetic resistance to diseases, insects, and even some kinds of poor weather.

The hybrids have enormous potential. Institute scientists have produced more than eight tons of rice in a single crop on one hectare (2.47 acres) of land. That is more than four times the average yield of a typical Asian farmer. Although farmers who have planted the hybrids fail to achieve such stupendous increases, many have doubled their yields, and some have managed as much as five tons per hectare. By 1975, perhaps a quarter or more of Asia's rice land had been planted with hybrids.

The degree of success, however, varies widely, often village by village and even farmer by farmer. Thus it is nearly impossible to make sweeping conclusions about the green revolution. Even so, it is clear that it has failed to live up to initial, if perhaps unreasonable, expectation. "We spoke of miracle rice like wonder bread," says Arturo Tanco, Jr., secretary of agriculture in the Philippines. "We were all far too optimistic on the basis of far too little experience."

Great expectations failed to allow for snags like bad weather, flaws in technology, and the difficulty of implementing anything new. Much of Asia was hungry in the 1960s. Much of Asia is still hungry in the 1970s. And the green revolution is meeting one of its greatest hurdles. Fertilizers and other chemicals have been priced out of reach of millions of farmers. Fertilizers are critical to the success of hybrid rices, and most of them are petroleum-based. In countries like India and Bangladesh, the unhappy choice is between importing food grains to feed hungry people now or importing fertilizer so that next year hungry people might be fed from increased domestic production. Understandably, fertilizer and next year's needs take second priority.

Even aside from fertilizer costs, some critics contend, the green revolution works to make rich farmers richer and poor farmers poorer, at least relatively. Certainly the farmer with more or better land, more education or management ability, and particularly more cash or credit for fertilizer and other materials is in a better position to exploit the hybrids. Some evidence in certain areas, such as northwest India, suggests a consequent increase in economic disparity and social tension. Yet the champions of the green revolution assert that it is up to governments to structure landholdings, credit systems exten- — sion services, and pricing policies in such a way that the mass of farmers can use the hybrids. "Scientists make the gains possible, technicians can make them practical, but politicians decide who gets them," says Ross of the rice institute.

That is as evident in the Philippines as anywhere else. Unlike Thailand, the Republic of the Philippines is not naturally rich in rice. Unlike Bangladesh, it is no international basket case. The country falls somewhere between these extremes. It was the first Asian nation to experiment with the green revolution, and it has the largest proportion of farmers, about 60 percent, planting hybrids. Yet, seven years after hybrid cultivation began to spread there in 1967, it was still growing insufficient rice to meet the demand of its 40 million people. Since then, the outlook has brightened, because the Philippines implemented what most experts think is a model program for making the technology of the green revolution available to the farmer in the paddy.

In the late 1960s there were experts who said that the Philippines had solved its rice problem. The first hybrid, IR-8, had spread rapidly through the country in 1967 and 1968. The weather was favorable, yields rose, and from 1969 to 1971 the Philippines for the first time in memory required no rice imports. "We already were looking for export markets," an official recalls.

In the fall of 1971 a series of storms struck the country. An outbreak of a rice disease to which IR-8 was vulnerable followed. Output slumped. In 1972 came the worst floods in Philippine history. The government had turned its attention from rice production to political and other economic matters. And of course the population was swelling, by more than 3 percent a year, as rice output fell and demand rose.

By 1973, the Philippines was struggling to avert famine. It bought foreign rice at exorbitant prices. Ration shops dispensed unappetizing mixtures of rice and coarse grains. People in cities were told to grow cabbage in their backyards.

Out of the crisis emerged a new national program called Masagana 99. *Masagana* means bountiful, and 99 is a target of 99 *cavanes*, or some 4.6 tons, of rice per hectare. The program is intended to reach 1.2 million hectares and enroll 500,000 farmers. By 1974, it had reached 900,000 hectares and enrolled 650,000 farmers. Before the program, average output on the targeted land was about 60 *cavanes;* by 1974, it had reached 78, according to the government.

Total Philippine rice output rose to 130 million tons in the 1974 crop year from 100 million tons in 1973. Production in 1973 was abnormally low because of the weather, but Masagana 99 helped make 1974 production a record. Even so, it failed to meet increased demand for 140 million tons, compared to 115 million in 1969, but the country was expected to become self-sufficient in rice production within a very few years.

Among the many reasons for the success of Masagana 99, two are critical. The program, first, was made a national priority. President Ferdinand Marcos publicly called it "a program of national survival" and personally supervised it. His secretary of agriculture, Tanco, gave it his undivided attention. Bureaucratic lethargy and red tape were kept from stifling the program. Second, the program was planned with care and common sense. It was tested on pilot plots in 1972 before being promoted nationally. Decentralized management left some decisions to the provincial and village levels. The focus and goals were oriented toward the individual farmer and his paddy rather than to nebulous national goals. Every farmer who enrolled has been entitled to a low-interest loan of 900 pesos, about $120, per hectare up to a total of five hectares. The loans have been provided by private rural banks or, in their absence in any area, by the Philippine National Bank. In remote areas, banks have gone out to farmers; Jeeps have brought credit supervisors and cashboxes. The loans have required no collateral, so that farmers have run no risk of losing their land or their water buffalo if crops failed.

Credit has been provided partly in cash and partly in chits that farmers take to stores and exchange for fertilizer, insecticides, and herbicides. Hybrid seeds have been made available through private and government channels. Government subsidies absorbed about half of a 350 percent rise in fertilizer prices over an 18-month period.

To educate farmers in hybrid-rice management, the government mounted a massive publicity campaign designed by J. Walter Thompson. Catch songs, jingles, and cartoons helped drive home the desirability of taking part in the yield-increase program. Daily radio programs have continued to advise farmers on technical matters, such as the application of pesticides. Chemical companies, profiting from the program, have helped promote it too.

Hybrid technology was condensed into 16 distinct steps to make it more easily comprehended and utilized by farmers. The government put into the field some 3,500 agricultural extension workers, all with college degrees in agriculture, to supervise and assist farmers enrolled in the program. The technicians also act as credit supervisors, and their incentive pay is related to the loan repayment rate of the farmers they assist.

Simple irrigation projects, like tube wells, pumps, and

small canals, have been encouraged. The government has earmarked development funds for major water-control projects. An effective national system of irrigation and water control will be expensive and time-consuming. But experts deem it necessary to consolidate the success of the green revolution. In the short term, the program has concentrated on land that already is irrigated, reducing the risk of failure. The government, meanwhile, has experimented with green-revolution agriculture on nonirrigated land.

For all this, Masagana has been troubled. World inflation has forced the government to increase credit allotments while reducing the volume of fertilizers and other materials. Insects and disease have frustrated control efforts. In 1974, floods damaged sizable areas in the program. There still are too few extension workers, and some of them do not fully understand hybrid agriculture themselves.

But talks with a score of farmers in a dozen barrios on Luzon appear to confirm the experts' opinion that Masagana 99 has a good chance to succeed permanently.

Very few of these farmers have managed 99 or more *cavanes* per hectare, but nearly all of them have achieved higher yields than they ever got before. Rudolfo Clemente, of the Gugo barrio, used to get about 50 *cavanes* from each of his three hectares. In 1974, he says, he averaged 105 *cavanes* per hectare. Florcencio Mallari, of Manginoo barrio, used to average 23 *cavanes* per hectare. In 1975, he got 45. His neighbor, Cornelio Masilang, has increased his yield to an average of 81 *cavanes* from 25. If the numbers vary widely, the trend is clearly upward.

Among the troubles are floodings, poor soil, and extra-large fertilizer requirements, lack of insecticides, and lack of gasoline for irrigation pumps. Still, the farmers who report these troubles, and other farmers, have been delighted with their higher yields. They have acknowledged that they got the credit they were promised and that they have been visited and assisted by government extension workers.

Still, farmers are conservative. And some have resisted joining the program. One is José Magla, who lives in Colgante barrio. He says he is perfectly happy with 50 *cavanes* of rice per hectare and happy to avoid worrying about new rice seeds, fertilizers, and loans to repay. Gabriel Manalastas, an elderly farmer in Manginoo barrio, hasn't joined because he wishes not to "bother the government." But the difficulty of obtaining fertilizer except through the program may, he concedes, force him to change his mind. "You better," his wife advises.

12

New Sources of Protein

Early in the 1970s, Department of Agriculture scientists began developing a curious new food. It was to be as rich in protein as a steak, but it would have no fat. It could be baked into bread and cookies, making them extranutritious. In raw form it would be a tasteless powder. But it could be given just about any flavor and texture.

This miracle food is the humble cottonseed.

The scientists' work has resulted in a maze of tubes and gadgets at the Plains Cooperative Oil Mill in the dusty West Texas city of Lubbock. The mill, owned by a cooperative of 15,000 cotton growers, has sunk nearly $4 million into a plant that turns cottonseed into high-protein flour. The assumption underlying this effort and investment is that the world's hungry will be as eager to eat cotton as to wear it. "We're the pioneers," plant manager John Herzer says. "We're tapping a completely new source of protein, and we're told that's where the real hunger is in the world today."

Indeed, there are hungry people in the world. But how can the cottonseed flour get to them? The Plains Cooperative is asking 35 cents a pound for its flour, putting it out of reach of people in many poor countries where spending 10 cents for a day's food can be extravagant. And most of the world's hungry live in technically unsophisticated countries that would find a cottonseed flour plant of their own a complex undertaking. Even the Lubbock cooperative struggled for more than a year to get its plant to work properly. India bought a similar plant. It has been beset with problems, and little if any flour has yet been produced.

Therein lies a cruel paradox. Although it is possible to turn previously inedible plants into nutritious food, the technology for doing so is too expensive and too complicated for the places where hunger is most acute. "This fancy technology is going to give greater choice to affluent people, but will do little to ease the needs of hungry people," a health official at the United Nations says. Joseph Hulse, a Canadian nutritionist, says that "probably the greatest obstacle to the transfer of technology is the serious shortage of relevant knowledge and experience existing in the developing countries."

Soybeans are the major source of new fabricated foods. Imitation sausages, ham, and chicken made from soybeans already are in supermarkets. Cottonseed will very likely be the next source. New foods from rapeseed and sunflower seed are in research and development. The most novel food source is the much-publicized single-cell protein—algae, bacteria, fungi, and yeasts that are fed on such materials as carbon dioxide, oil, and natural gas to produce a protein-rich microbial cell mass.

Microbial protein is intended for cattle and poultry food. "Any large-scale use for human food is a long way off," says Harold Rice, a nutrition adviser to the Agency for International Development. Still, there is some hope that microbial protein can help ease hunger in poor countries on a small scale within a few years. Researchers in the United States and England are trying to develop simple vats in which low-protein foods such as cassava (tapioca) could be fermented into a high-protein food. Inexpensive and uncomplicated vats might be usable in even the poorest of villages for making food.

Because so many countries lack skilled labor and capital, some researchers are concentrating on nutritious subsistence crops that can thrive under the care of the humblest backcountry farmer and that can be processed easily into food. Thus new foods in much of the developing world are likely to come from a rugged hybrid plant called triticale or from bread made from such grains as millet, a protein-rich sorghum. The Agency for International Development and Canada's International Development Research Center have funded international teams researching ways to increase the acreage of crops that agricultural scientists previously ignored: cereal crops such as sorghum and millet and legumes such as chick peas, cow peas, and pigeon peas.

Sorghum is especially promising because of the recent discoveries of two Ethiopian strains that contain three times as much protein as other types. The two Purdue University scientists who found the strains are cautious, however. They say that much work remains before seed stocks can be developed for distribution to farmers. Meanwhile, the Canadian research center is financing studies on making bread from wheat flour combined with sorghum or millet flour to conserve wheat.

Triticale is far more advanced. It is a cross between wheat and rye. It is higher in protein than wheat. It is rugged enough to grow where other crops cannot. It dates back to the nineteenth century. The first cross between wheat and rye was reported in 1876 by a Scottish scientist. But it remained a laboratory curiosity until 1937, when a French scientist demonstrated its potential as a food crop. Since then, the slow process of breeding has resulted in bigger yields.

A number of countries have tested triticale, and it may become the first "new" plant ever to become a significant food crop. Rice of the Agency for International Development thinks, however, that farmers in developing countries will be slow to accept it. "Triticale is simply too strange in appearance and taste," he says. He believes that new high-protein sorghums are likely to gain acceptance long before triticale because sorghum is a familiar crop.

Under way are laboratory efforts to breed new high-protein cereal crops from crosses of more than two species. But this work is in its infancy. It could be decades before any viable varieties emerge. The only other new crop that promises to help end malnutrition is a high-protein corn called Opaque 2.

Although it was developed ten years ago, it still has not reached the world's hungry. The kernel has been too soft for milling. A new Opaque 2 with a harder kernel recently has been developed and tested. Such cereal crops, however, produce only limited amounts of protein. For this reason the most elaborate research involves a class of vegetables called legumes, which have the highest protein content. The oilseeds, prized for their oil and popular as animal feed, have the most of all. Oilseeds such as soybeans and cottonseed can be turned into foods that taste something like meat, milk, and cheese. And as meat prices climb, Department of Agriculture nutritionist Kermit Bird believes, "this country will be forced to make the transition from a primarily animal-protein food economy to one in which plant proteins attain a greater degree of importance."

Bird estimates that two thirds of food protein in the United States come from animal meat and animal products. "In another several decades," he says, "I believe we will be obtaining one half to two thirds of our food-grade proteins from plant-derived sources." Frost and Sullivan, a New York research firm, estimates than 3.89 billion pounds of soy protein alone will be used in foods by 1980, compared with 300 million pounds in 1972.

Kurt Konigsbacher calls this a "second revolution" in food. He formerly was with the Foster D. Shell subsidiary of Booz, Allen and Hamilton. In his view, the first revolution occurred in the last century when the mass movement of people from country to city began and more fresh food had to be processed by canning, pasteurizing, and, later, by freezing. Now, he says, the second revolution, doing away with the big family meal and elevating snacking, is taking place. "By taking the basic building blocks, such as soybean protein, and changing them into any shape or form we need, snacks can become nutritious foods," he says.

Much work needs to be done. A. S. Clausi, research director for General Foods Corporation, observes that vegetable proteins as food still present "unresolved texture and flavor problems." Texture has been more easily imitated than taste. General Mills' Country Cuts "chicken" cubes and "ham" cubes and Miles Laboratories' Morningstar Farms "sausage" links and patties and "ham" slices imitate the texture of the real thing with remarkable fidelity. But their flavor clearly is a problem. The chicken tastes of chemicals, and the flavor of sausage is barely detectable through a larding of spices. Only soybean protein goes into these imitations now. In a few years, however, cottonseed-based imitations may be on the market. Baking companies already are using some cotton-seed flour to fortify cereals and baked goods.

The cottonseed kernel contains a toxic substance called gossypol, an appetite depressant in humans. Since it does not affect cattle, cottonseed has long been used for animal feed after the oil has been removed. The only way to make cotton-seed fit for human consumption, until recently, was to destroy the gossypol by cooking the kernel. That also destroyed much of the protein. Then in the late 1960s, researchers at the Department of Agriculture's research laboratory in New Orleans found that the sac containing gossypol could be floated out of the kernel with the solvent hexane. After removal of the hard seed hull, the seed is ground into large granules and mixed with hexane. The resulting slurry goes into a centrifuge machine called a liquid cyclone that separates the granules from the gossypol sacs.

At the cottonseed-flour plant in Lubbock there are refinements. After the gossypol-free slurry has left the cyclone machine, it passes through a filter that removes its oil, then through a device that removes the hexane odor and finally through a flour mill. (A variety of cotton that is free of gossypol is under development in Texas. Its seeds could be ground conventionally into flour.

Rapeseed, another high-protein oilseed, also is toxic. The toxicity comes from chemicals called glucosinolates. A commercial plant for removing the glucosinolates is being built in Canada in Sexsmith, Alberta. Using a new Swedish process that removes the toxin with water, the plant is expected to produce about 5,000 tons a year of 65 percent rapeseed flour.

Generations of children have cracked sunflower seeds between their teeth, but the flour made from the seeds turns bright green in even slightly alkaline water because of the seed's chlorogenic acid. A process for washing out this acid could lead to sunflower-seed flour, too.

Most of these protein-rich oilseeds are grown in the poorest countries of Africa and Asia. But these countries generally export the crops as oil or cattlefeed in return for badly needed foreign exchange. And they lack the technical ability to make flour from the crops.

13

A Change in Habits

The eating habits of a nation develop and change slowly, except in extraordinary times. These seem to be such times. Food consumption patterns in the United States are changing more than at any other time since the Great Depression. This time the change may be more lasting, and the implications may extend beyond the food industry.

For years the industry considered it noteworthy if the annual volume of a particular food rose or fell by more than 5 percent. A 5 percent change these days is likely to be considered evidence of outstanding stability. Specific figures are hard to come by, partly because some corporations prefer not to reveal how chancy things really are. But those figures that are available, along with the observations of food executives, point to this conclusion: After years of looking for the quick and easy way to eat, Americans are going back to basics.

"Today's consumers," says Donald S. Perkins, chairman of Jewel Companies, the supermarket chain, "are willing to do it themselves."

That means more than merely passing up all the heat-and-eat goodies found in American stores. It means, for example, home baking: 60 percent of the respondents in one survey said they baked their own bread; 26 percent stated that they did it regularly. Many other types of cooking from scratch also are increasing.

Other trends include an upswing in lunchtime brown bagging, home gardening, and canning and storing of food in anticipation of shortages or higher prices. A survey shows that the weekly steak no longer is a priority item among working-class families. The casserole appears entrenched as the all-American meal. Inside the supermarket, shoppers are relying more faithfully on lists of what they truly need and resisting impulse buying with remarkable vigor.

All this means surprisingly large increases or decreases in volume for a large number of food products. Among the significant losers are convenience foods. According to an estimate, unit sales of canned meat, fish, and poultry products are down anywhere from 25 percent to 60 percent, depending on the item, from their peaks of the early 1970s.

Frozen foods, likewise, whose volume had boomed for years, are believed to be down sharply. A spokesman for the American Frozen Food Institute says that meaningful volume comparisons are not readily calculable. But Jewel Companies, whose figures are probably typical, says its frozen prepared-food volume fell 16 percent in one year, 1974. Other notable losers are thought to be cake and some other baking mixes, canned fruits and vegetables, desserts, and ready-to-eat snacks of all kinds.

On the other hand, some products are racking up strong gains. A significant one is family flour, the kind bought in five-pound and ten-pound packages. After declining for twenty consecutive years, per-capita consumption of family flour rose in 1973 and again in 1974, by 10 percent in the latter year. Other basic ingredients also have shown above-normal increases. Jewel Companies says its baking-soda unit volume rose 28 percent in 1974, dry yeast 32 percent, and sugar 17 percent. "We haven't seen anything like this since 1932 or 1933," says Wallace N. Rasmussen, president of the foods division of Beatrice Foods Company.

Why? The late recession certainly offers part of the explanation. Food prices rose by nearly 30 percent in 1973–1974, and they were still climbing when millions of Americans were being thrown out of work. When delaying or canceling purchases of new cars or television sets failed to halt the slide in family fortunes, the ax fell on the food budget. Many food-industry officials say that buying eventually will return to normal.

But some analysts of consumer behavior think that this tells only part of the story. Population trends, the cost of energy, and world hunger are playing a role, and they think that America's food-buying habits may not return to "normal" for a very long time. Many among the nation's wives and mothers, moreover, the people who say the most about what America eats, echo this view. "A lot of people I know just aren't planning to go back to the old ways," says Mrs. Grace Pakata of Park Forest, Illinois.

Better Homes and Gardens, in a late 1974 survey, found that 63 percent of respondents agreed with the proposition that they were making "important and lasting changes" in the way they shop and dine.*

Any sustained change has implications for the way of life of the entire nation. "Eating has as much to say about who we are and how we live as anything," observes Paul Fine, a New York psychologist who has done food-consumption studies. "What happens is that families start cutting back for economic reasons. But at some point, and we're not quite sure when it starts, but it has, people's whole way of thinking and their lifestyle start to change. They begin to realize they can get along without a lot of things formerly considered necessities."

The makeup of the population may have something to do with changing consumption patterns. Thanks to the baby boom after World War II, demographers note, the American population has been tilting toward the age group of twenty- to early-thirty-year-olds. Some social scientists consider that people in their twenties are making critical choices that may change the nation's lifestyle.

It should be stressed, however, that not all experts agree. "I don't buy this 'nonconsumption lifestyle' stuff," says analyst

---

* The survey formed part of a series of nine articles entitled "A Report to the Food Industry" which the magazine published between December 1973 and April 1975.

Ben Wattenberg. "I don't see that these wonderful children of ours are averse to spending money."

Nevertheless, some people in their twenties and early thirties clearly share attitudes and beliefs different from those held by earlier generations. "The war babies are thirty years old and on a diet," says Mary Elberty, a commodities analyst for Drexel, Burnham and Company, the brokers. "All those fun, fancy, and convenient foods don't fit the mentality of people today. Gimmicky things won't sell anymore." Even working wives seem to be cutting back on convenience foods. *Better Homes and Gardens* says that about 40 percent of the respondents in its survey were working wives. "Though they're slightly more inclined to use convenience foods than their counterparts who stay at home, the biggest news about their habits is that there isn't much difference," says publisher Jack D. Rehm.

Some respondents made the point rather forcefully. One woman wrote that even though she works full-time, she cooks "the way I cooked when we had three children and I didn't work—more casseroles, more soups, more from-scratch food."

Aside from other economic and social trends, the increased cost of energy may have had a deep effect on food all of its own. Concern over energy has implanted conservation firmly in the American consciousness. A study commissioned by the Super Market Institute in 1974 concluded that "the gasoline shortage has left a long-lasting imprint on the American public—they believe that shortages can and do happen."

Nobody seriously expects the United States suddenly to become unable to feed its population, even though getting adequate amounts of food from the field to the tables of some poorer Americans remains difficult to achieve. Still, growing concern over hunger and America's role in easing it has moved a number of Americans to question their own eating habits. One young mother wrote, in response to a study commissioned by *Family Circle,* that "society cannot afford a world that eats like America does. I think we are going to have to accept a change in our way of living and eating—not just 'until the crisis is over' but for good."*

* Published by *Family Circle Magazine* in 1975 in a booklet entitled "Today's Supermarket Shopper."

14

The Grim Progression

Today—during this one day—the world's population will increase by some 200,000 people, the size of a Des Moines or a Salt Lake City or a Grand Rapids. Tomorrow there will be a similar increase, and the next day. And the next. And the next, for many years to come.

So goes the grim progression that threatens to overcrowd the globe and strain its ability to feed, clothe, and shelter its inhabitants. "The magnitude of the new population boom surpasses all earlier expectations," warns a United Nations report on the long-range implications of world population growth. "The longer the high tempo persists . . . the more precarious will be prospects for a healthy life on this planet."*

Most experts anticipate that by the year 2000, the world's population, now 4 billion, will approach 6.5 billion. And if certain assumptions go awry, the twenty-first century could dawn on a globe with well over 7 billion inhabitants—as many as 2 million more than were expected by forecasters in 1966. "The question is not, 'Will the world's population grow?' but

* United Nations Department of Economic and Social Affairs, "Concise Report on the World Population Situation in 1970–1975 and Its Long-Range Implications," *Population Studies Series*, No. 56, New York, 1974.

'Under what conditions will it stop?' " says Samuel Baum, supervisory statistician for international demographic research at the Bureau of the Census.

Present attempts at restraint are being overwhelmed. The world's average birth rate is declining as more and more nations emphasize population control. Yet the global death rate has been falling even more rapidly because of improved living conditions and the conquest of disease.

While population growth in the industrial nations of the West is slowing significantly, massive increases are continuing in the developing regions of the world: Latin America, Africa, and Asia. In the more primitive lands, birthrates are now three times as high as in the industrialized nations of North America and Europe. Mexico, with less than one third the population of the United States, adds as many people—1.9 million—to it each year as this country does. Most demographers are not sanguine about the outlook in the less developed countries. "It's difficult for me to see any dramatic reduction in the growth rate in Africa, Asia, and Latin America," says Frederick A. Leedy, supervisory statistician for international program planning evaluation at the Bureau of the Census.

Unquestionably, by the close of this century, the world's population burden will tend to shift from the industrial nations of the North to the more rural, developing nations of the South. North America, Europe, and other developed regions, now growing at the rate of less than 1 percent a year, are expected to increase by only some 200 million people. Expanding more than twice as rapidly, Africa, Asia, and South America are expected to add 2 billion inhabitants. By the year 2000, four fifths of the world's population will be concentrated in the developing countries; the proportion now is less than three quarters.

Population densities will increase almost everywhere, particularly in South Asia. The pressures will produce unprecedented problems for the less developed regions of the world, even threatening the survival of some nations. In 1966, the *Wall Street Journal* reported a tentative conclusion that "birth-control programs are making headway in some of the lands whose population problems are most acute." And it ap-

peared then that even the large population growth still anticipated was unlikely "to lead to mass starvation or other catas-
trophes." Today, demographers are much less optimistic.

If nothing worse, analysts foresee a spread of reactionary
regimes. "Faced with increasingly difficult problems brought
on in part by population growth, governments are bound to
take a firm hand to bring them under control. The rights of the
individual will have to give way to the rights of the community," a State Department population specialist maintains.

But more than the spread of authoritarian governments,
forecasters fear the growth of conflicts within or between
densely populated countries. They find omens for the future in
the recent past. Nazli Choucri, a Massachusetts Institute of
Technology political scientist, has analyzed the causes of
ninety-three conflicts in or between developing nations in the
years 1945 to 1969. She concludes that population pressures
played a significant role in sixty-six, including the Algerian
war for independence, the Nigeria-Biafra conflict, and the
Mideast war of 1973. "The higher the rate of growth, the more
salient a factor population increase appears to be in the development of conflict and violence," she contends.*

Particular problems arise from patterns of immigration.
Kuwait, for example, has imported 70 percent of its work force,
and there is tension between native citizens and the foreign-
born, who have fewer rights. Mexico's large population growth
and sparse economic opportunity produce a steady flow of il-
legal migrants into the southwestern United States; they are
becoming a major source of this country's population increase.
"It can't get anything but worse," says Justin Blackwelder,
president of the Environmental Fund, a population-control
group that advocates stricter curbs on immigration.

Urban growth probably will continue undiminished into
the next century, creating huge megalopolises. By 2000, some
50 percent of the world's population is expected to live in
urban areas, compared with 39 percent now. The trend will be
particularly marked in the developing lands, where urban

Population Dynamics and International Violence (Indianapolis: D. C.
Heath & Co., 1974), p. 104.

growth rates are now more than twice as high as in the industrialized countries. By the turn of the century, demographers calculate, there will be at least 60 cities with 5 million or more people, compared with the current twenty-one. Mexico City, now third-ranking, is expected to swell into the world's largest metropolitan area with 31.5 million inhabitants.

This surge of urbanization will be spurred by better communications, transportation, and industrialization. Rural residents will continue to be pushed from the countryside by poverty and pulled to the cities by hopes of jobs and money. Population planners worry that this vast displacement of the poor will intensify the difficulties of accommodating the huge total increase in mankind.

"What is new about the situation [urbanization] in developing areas today is not poverty per se, but its massiveness, its potentiality for increase, its incongruous association with high technology, and its rapidly eroding opportunity for alleviation," declares Kingsley Davis, a demographer at the University of California.

On average, the populations of most developing nations will remain young, because of high birthrates. In the year 2000, it is expected, nearly half their inhabitants will still be below the age of twenty. The demand for education and jobs will be tremendous.

Moreover, there will be many women yet to enter their child-bearing years. Thus, even if births dropped rapidly to the replacement level of two children per family, population growth would continue for another seventy to eighty years in developing lands, the experts calculate. The average family size in those countries now is more than twice the replacement level. Though population may cease growing by the end of the century in North America and Europe, elsewhere "such an achievement is most unlikely and probably impossible," declares Tomas Frejka, a demographer with the Population Council, a leader in population research.

The momentum in world population growth became grimly clear to demographers more than a decade ago. Experts then noted that birthrates were rising and mortality was falling in the developing lands. The long-range projections made in the 1960s were not much lower than those made today. But the totals remain similar only because of a happy coincidence of forecasting miscalculations. Some nations grew more slowly than expected. Others grew faster.

China, the world's most populous nation, was thought in the early 1960s to be growing as rapidly as the rest of Asia. Many population experts assumed that its birthrate was higher than 35 births per 1,000 population and would drop only a few points in the next decade. (The United States rate was then 22.5 and since has dropped to 17.) But now the message carried out from behind the Bamboo Curtain by most visitors is that China's birthrate has dropped by perhaps 10 points because of the Communist regime's emphasis on family planning. Within another ten years, China's birthrate could be lower than this country's, says Dr. Reimert Ravenholt, who heads the Agency for International Development's family planning programs abroad.

China embarked on population control in the mid-1950s. While Chairman Mao appeared at first to waver in his commitment, family planning is now an article of political faith in Peking. "China's is probably the most clearly emphasized and sponsored program in the world," says John Aird, head of the Department of Commerce's foreign demographic analysis division.

The two-child family is the Chinese goal, except for sparsely settled mountain areas where a larger labor force is needed. Visitors report that local communes set birth quotas and decide which couples can have children each year. Delay in marriage to the age of twenty-eight for men and twenty-five for women is emphasized. All forms of contraception, including the Chinese version of the pill, a drug-impregnated soluble paper dissolved in the mouth, are made widely available.

Many China specialists attribute the family planning successes more to the unusual nature of the Chinese society. "China's rural population is different from other developing countries," say Leo Orlans, a Library of Congress authority. "It's better educated. The women are employed and have a more important role in decision making and society."

For most other developing nations, demographers now

admit that they were unduly optimistic that modern medical technology could rapidly reduce birthrates. Only in a few of the smaller countries, such as Taiwan, South Korea, and Greenland, have sharp declines occurred. In a span of eight years, Greenland's birthrate was cut by more than half, to 19.5 per 1,000. But there's little evidence of success in nations with massive population reservoirs, particularly India, Pakistan, and Bangladesh. "In the past . . . people felt with the technological breakthrough [in contraceptive methods] they would control world fertility in a decade; now there is a period of reassessment," notes Shigemi Kono, a United Nations demographer.

More than two decades ago, India embarked on an intensive population control program, and the United States' aid program made reduction of India's birthrate a prime goal. But the rate has fallen only a few points, and India's population growth remains among the highest in the world. At 600 million now, the subcontinent's population could exceed 1.1 billion in the year 2000 and could eventually surpass China's. Most demographers attribute the apparent failure in India partly to the government's ineptitude and to prejudice against the pill based on health concerns. But most of the trouble lies in the nature of Indian society, they say. Among the influences that help sustain the high birthrate are early marriage, Hinduism's emphasis on bearing sons, dependence on children for security in old age, and a low level of education among the rural masses.

There is no doubt that birth control slows population growth. But its impact has been felt mainly in the developed nations. Many experts argue that modern contraception can accelerate a birthrate decline that is already under way, but will not actually start a downtrend. So population planners increasingly are abandoning their emphasis on medical solutions to world population growth and focusing on longer-range remedies in social and economic development. Demographers note that birthrates tend to fall when income increases and is more evenly distributed, when education is more widespread, and when more women become part of the work force.

And even though the decline in the world's death rate has

contributed to population growth, experts argue that reduction of death rates is essential for lowering birthrates in developing countries. So long as infant mortality is high, they reason, parents will insist on having large numbers of offspring. In India, where the average life expectancy is thirty-seven years, parents must have six children to insure that one lives to their old age.

But in fact the death rate decline has leveled off in the developing nations of Asia and Africa. And during the past three years, death rates have actually risen in India, Bangladesh, Sri Lanka (formerly Ceylon), and the Sahelian regions south of the Sahara in Africa, according to Lester Brown, president of Worldwatch Institute, a research organization dealing with population and other issues.

Brown reasons that the rise in deaths stems largely from huge price increases in wheat, rice, and other basic foodstuffs. Nutrition suffered in impoverished lands where people devote 50 percent to 80 percent of their income to food. The effect on women and children has been particularly severe; infant mortality rates have risen rapidly, reports Irene Tinker, director of the Office of International Science at the American Association for the Advancement of Science.

Some optimistic planners insist that world growth rates will be cut in half within a decade and the total population by the turn of the century kept well under 5.5 billion. But there are many ifs:

—If India, Pakistan, and Bangladesh, after years of futile efforts, curb their rate of population increase.

—If African and Latin American nations, which may double their populations before the year 2000, admit they have growth problems and take action. At the World Population Conference in Bucharest last year, representatives of many of these nations argued that population growth was desirable and insisted that redistribution of wealth, not population control, would resolve their difficulties.

—If new superquick methods of sterilizing men and women in out-patient clinics bring the hoped-for results. Experts at the Agency for International Development say that more than 100 operations can be performed daily by one doctor, and they say that 10,000 clinics at a cost of $100 million would meet the needs of Africa, Latin America, and Asia. Along with the other uncertainties, demographers concede that they have only a rough knowledge of the size of the world's current population. In some countries of Africa and Asia, a census never has been taken or is badly out of date. In others, like Nigeria, the figures are suspected of inflation for political reasons. The major uncertainty centers on China. The last full-scale census, taken in 1953, showed its population at 583 million. There is sharp disagreement among China experts on the growth since then. UN experts estimate the current population at 838 million. But the Department of Commerce's John Aird, who doubts that birthrates have dropped much, believes that China's population is between 925 million and 1.1 billion. He expects it to rise by the year 2000 to as high as 1.5 billion, far more than other forecasters expect. Thus China remains a demographic puzzle. The Chinese have consistently refused visitors access to their birth and death records in Peking. American experts believe China's rulers themselves do not know how big the population is.

While little can be done to resolve the huge uncertainty about China, the United States and the UN are financing a survey to improve data on many other parts of the world. By the time it is completed in 1981, the project will provide better information on fertility in seventy nations, helping to show the impact of family planning programs on birthrates. But neither this information nor the control efforts now being made can offer assurance of reducing the number of people that may crowd the planet in another quarter-century.

15

Egypt versus Babies

Mustafa el Enani is the handsome, relaxed moderator of "The Happy Home" program on Egyptian television. It is a talk show, and el Enani questions guests about their love life, the size of their families, and their attitudes toward the pill. He loads his patter with plugs for birth control, ending with a punch line: "The small family is the happy family." At the program's close, the camera focuses on a wall poster. A cartoon portrays a newly married couple, the mustached groom grinning rakishly, the bride demure in her wedding gown. The Arabic script reads: "When you are married, remember that two are better . . ." There are two pictures. The first is of two smiling babies. The second is of six squalling brats. The caption under the latter continues: ". . . than this."

As this suggests, Egypt is eager to have smaller families. It is a goal in other parts of the world, too, especially in some poverty-stricken nations. The prospect that the world's population of some 4 billion people may nearly double by 2010 appalls many demographers, economists, food-aid administrators, and national planners. There is no certainty that there will be enough food and other resources to care for that many people. Unless steps are taken soon to bring population growth under control, the third world of developing nations faces economic stagnation, massive unemployment, hunger, disease, political unrest, and war. "Overpopulation is a problem in developing countries because it adversely affects economic development," says Dr. Aziz Bindary, the Sorbonne philosopher and gynecologist who is chairman of Egypt's council for family planning.

Egypt is a prime example. It has a population of 36 million, expanding at a 2 percent annual rate. This puts the country on an economic treadmill. As fast as its gross national product rises, new bodies appear to claim a share of the nation's goods and services, so per-capita income rises very slowly.

The situation is common throughout the third world. The figures of the expanding worldwide population mask some important distortions. Populations are rising only .9 percent a year in richer, developed nations with high standards of living. The rise is 2.4 percent a year in poverty-stricken lands that have trouble supporting the people they have now. "The rich are getting richer, while the poor are getting poorer, because the population now is increasing more than twice as fast in the poor nations as it is in the rich countries," an official of the United Nations' Food and Agriculture Organization in Rome observes.

The widening dichotomy creates some grim situations in parts of the world. In Mauritius, the lush, green island in the Indian Ocean, only one in every five students who finish school can find a job. In India, a million more mouths a month are clamoring for food as the "green revolution" of crop expansion seems to have spent its force. Uncontrolled population growth in poor lands has pushed the estimated total in the less developed world from 2 billion people in 1960 to more than 2.75 billion in 1974. In rich, developed nations the total rose from 1 billion to just over 1.1 billion in the same period.

Population is soaring primarily because of improvements in health and sanitation in recent decades. One UN demographer says, "People used to breed like rabbits and die like flies. Now life expectancies have been greatly increased. But in the rich, developed countries fertility rates declined, too, and the population problem is minimal. In developing countries, the same old high fertility rates are being maintained, and there are many more people breeding."

Nevertheless, family planning, particularly as the only method of dealing with the population problem, remains very controversial. On the one hand are those who swear by family planning, citing figures on births "averted" as enthusiastically as generals used to announce body counts in the Vietnam war. A few countries go to great lengths to encourage their citizens to practice family planning. Singapore, for example, is making headway in reducing its fertility rate by enforcing "social disincentives," including punitive prenatal and delivery fees and low priority in housing for parents who have more than three children. Singapore also promotes and frequently finances sterilization procedures and abortions.

In most other countries, governments do not participate so actively in family planning and sometimes stay out of it altogether, relying instead on private efforts. However, a World Bank study predicts that "within a decade or two perhaps half the governments of the world will be offering family-planning services as a routine public service designed to influence the size and growth" of their populations.

Between the extremes is the thesis that family planning should be promoted along with other programs for economic development. In very poor nations, parents often regard extra children as possibly valuable workhands for the future and as extra insurance for their own care in old age. Rising industrial production and agricultural output themselves encourage people to have smaller families. Parents experiencing a rising standard of living are more likely to view children as an economic liability.

"If there is no pie to split, it doesn't make much difference to parents how many children are standing around by the empty pie tin," says an Egyptian social worker. "It is only when the pie is there that advantages of the smaller family become evident to parents." Dr. Bindary says, "A population plan has to relate itself to a total socioeconomic plan, for population growth should be a function and a variable of the total plan."

Egypt's problems are not unique in the developing world.

Like India, it is pushing family planning hard along with its economic development. Today, there are in Egypt some 3,000 government and 520 private clinics providing birth control information and dispensing pills and contraceptives at subsidized prices. Dr. Bindary says that some social workers now employ "face-to-face communications, what the Hoover company did fifty years ago and called door-to-door selling." As in some sales campaigns, doctors and others working in the field are paid commissions according to the number of intrauterine contraceptive devices inserted in women.

Television and radio carry the message. Program moderator el Enani reports that he has no difficulty inducing Egyptian men and women to appear on programs to reveal intimate details of their sex lives. "Once in a while you encounter a reticent chap," he says, but "usually people like to appear on television to talk about themselves."

Some "births averted" progress has been made. Since the birth control campaign was started in 1966, the annual rate of population gain has dropped from 2.5 percent to just under 2 percent. But Dr. Bindary does not think the deliberate planning accounted for the entire drop. War played a part, as did increased prosperity in some families. But, as a visit to some of the populous villages along the Nile shows, much remains to be done to encourage family planning.

The land is flat, with green fields wedged between unreclaimed desert and occasional stands of date palms. Brown canals bring the Nile's water to soil that yields four crops of vegetables a year. In one field, a *fellah*, or peasant, tills the soil with a camel and a water buffalo yoked together. A woman in black, her face veiled, trudges along a dirt road, balancing a clay pot on her head. Children swim in one of the canals, laughing and shouting. A hot, bright sun beats down, and the pigeons sitting atop the cubelike mud huts of one village seem too listless to fly. But Omar Mohammed, a mustached *fellah* in a long gownlike *gallabieh*, seems cheerfully oblivious of the heat.

He also seems cheerfully oblivious of family planning. He boasts to a visitor of his twelve children. In the earthen compound of his home, he lays his hand on the shaven head of an eleven-year-old and says, "This is Yusef." The boy, who is studying English in school, frowns. "I mean, Ibrahim," the father quickly corrects himself. The frown deepens and the father loses his composure. "Ah, no, it is Abdullah," he says apologetically. The children are growing so fast, Omar Mohammed explains, that he cannot keep track of them.

Not far away is the town of Mit-Rahina, ancient Memphis, capital of lower Egypt 3,000 years before Christ. Little physically remains from that period, but local customs are deeply rooted in the old ways. "The people have a tradition of large families," says Dr. Awatif Abdulla, a woman physician who manages the local fourteen-bed hospital. "We must break down that tradition." It will take some doing. Though several hundred women usually attend the birth-control lectures given in the town hall near the hospital, Dr. Abdulla says that only some sixty women are actually planning their families. That would hardly make a dent in the population explosion. Mit-Rahina had about 10,000 people in 1974, up from 7,000 in 1967, and the average family has about five living children.

In an agricultural area like this, children mean more field hands. Thus it is difficult to persuade a *fellah* that he might be better off with two instead of ten children. And because parents expect to spend their old age with any surviving children, a large family helps insure that at least one or two of the children will outlive their parents.

"A small family may mean a lonely old age," says a grizzled resident of thirty-eight who looks closer to sixty years old. Of ten children, he has seven still living as his old-age insurance.

None of the *fellahin* hereabouts are wealthy, even by their own modest standards, but Saad Mahmoud is better off than most. He has five acres planted in cotton, corn, and vegetables and a grove of 300 date palms. "I can support my children very well," he says. He has eight. Six of them are daughters, ranging in age from eight to twenty years. Saad Mahmoud worries about marrying them off, but he wants all of them to finish school first. Though he does not think of it this way, completing their education would foster a slowdown in the birth rate. Girls in the village have been marrying at ages from fourteen to eighteen and sometimes even younger, boys at eighteen to twenty-one. As children attend school longer, they marry older. More than 40 percent of Mit-Rahina's residents are under fifteen. With women and the aged, some developing lands now have dependency ratios exceeding 80 percent, meaning that less than 20 percent of the population must support the rest.

16

An Ounce of Prevention

Looking ahead just twenty-four years to the year 2000, medical experts are certain of dramatic advances that will vanquish some of today's worst health scourges and lessen the fearful consequences of others. But they are just as certain of something that may seem paradoxical: Nothing that emerges from a clinic or a test tube will contribute nearly as much to better health generally as a little individual self-care in the form of wiser living. More than anything else, the growing acceptance of that view has changed the current outlook for health advances from the prospect envisioned by health experts in 1966.

Since 1966, medical research and development has progressed. Today, Americans get more and better medical care than they did, and they will continue to get it. But the returns from scientific advances are diminishing. Health authorities believe that more doctors and hospitals, more and more expensive machines for diagnosis and treatment, and new drugs and vaccines will have no more effect on good health overall than self-imposed changes in the way people live.

"The individual," says Dr. John H. Knowles, president of the research-oriented Rockefeller Foundation, "must realize that a perpetuation of the present system of high-cost, after-the-fact medicine will only result in higher costs and more frustration. The next major advance in the health of the American people will result only from what the individual is willing to do for himself."

Consider cancer and heart disease. It has become clear that neither is "caught" like a cold. Instead, both usually arise after decades of abuse of the body. Years of heavy smoking or drinking, high-fat diets, obesity, and lack of regular exercise have been shown to play a role. Yet all these causes can be moderated or eliminated without medical treatment. Knowles asserts that many Americans have come to look on "sloth, gluttony, alcoholic intemperance, reckless driving, sexual frenzy, and smoking" as constitutional rights, and they have come to expect government-financed "cures" for all the unhappy consequences. "But one man's freedom," he says, "is another man's shackles in taxes and insurance premiums. Meanwhile, the people have been led to believe that national health insurance, more doctors, and greater use of high-cost, hospital-based technologies will improve health. Unfortunately, none of them will."

In 1975, the country's health bill rose by more than $14 billion to $118.5 billion, or 8.3 percent of the gross national product. The federal government's share of the bill, through Medicare, Medicaid, and other health programs, jumped by 22.2 percent. Less than 3 percent of this spending went toward the prevention of disease. By far the greatest part went to treat existing ailments. Small wonder, then, that health experts are trying to promote preventive medicine. And by 2000, most doctors are likely to practice within publicly or privately financed health-maintenance organizations oriented as much toward preventive medicine as toward clinical treatment.

Because insurance companies and government are financing an ever-increasing share of medical expenses, the outlook is for much closer control over costs, including doctors' fees, drugs, equipment, and hospital care. There may be a closer monitoring of the quality of care given by doctors and institutions. It is even possible, despite the fierce opposition of doctors today, that health care will be completely socialized by 2000.

More effective treatment of cancer and heart disease would greatly increase the life span of many Americans actually suffering from those ailments. Overall, however, not even a sharp reduction in cancer and heart deaths would prolong the average life by much. A 25 percent reduction in mortality from heart disease, statisticians at the Metropolitan Life Insurance Company estimate, would increase the average life of forty-five-year-old males by sixteen months, of females of the same age by fourteen months. A 25 percent reduction in cancer mortality would extend male life expectancy by seven months, female by only five months. Such reductions in mortality from cancer, heart disease, and other ailments are possible and even probable, health specialists say. Here is the outlook in specific health categories:

Cancer. It is really more than 100 different diseases with a common denominator, the uncontrolled proliferation of abnormal cells. Of the trillions of cells that make up a human body, a few always are "going wild." The body's sophisticated immunity system normally detects these cells and does away with them. In cancer patients, the immunity system appears either unable to detect the maverick cells or unable to eliminate them.

Thus, strengthening the natural immunity system offers a strategy for defeating cancer. By 2000, specialists believe, the tactics should be perfected. As today, doctors still will rely on a combination—immunotherapy, radiotherapy, chemotherapy, and surgery. More cancer patients will be treated at specialized centers where the most effective methods can be employed. The search for substances that compensate for a cancer patient's faulty immunity system is already under way, and by 2000 the dangerous side effects of such substances may well have been moderated.

Some current research is devoted to identifying a substance secreted by growing tumors that appears to cause the body to create a set of blood vessels to nourish the tumor. By 2000, researchers may have identified this substance and developed a chemical defense against it.

Basic research in the functioning of cells is likely to produce therapeutic advances by 2000. Among them will be exquisitely sensitive methods for detecting cancer at its earliest stages, when treatment is most likely to be effective. The fast-growing store of information on the genetic, environmental, and dietary factors involved in many kinds of cancer also will help doctors treat patients earlier. A "national registry of cancer-prone families" was recently proposed. By 2000, it could be compiled and made useful for doctors and patients. Specialists think some cancer, too, is preventable by the elimination of suspect chemicals from the environment, including work places, and from food and drink.

Cardiovascular disease. With more than one million deaths attributed to them last year, heart disease and afflictions of the blood vessels now are the leading killers. Cardiovascular disease will remain the main cause of death in 2000. Like cancer, it occurs after decades of abuse, so that many people not yet middle-aged are dooming themselves to the ailment. That is not to say that there will not be striking advances in treatment. And certainly, more will be known about the precise role of high-fat diets, smoking, lack of exercise, and emotional temperament in cardiovascular disease.

Specially trained medical teams for emergency heart cases already are employed in many hospitals. The teams will be more readily available to the average American by 2000. Drugs that limit heart damage in a heart attack will be more widely used, too. And doctors probably will have perfected procedures for using blood-vessel transplants and other surgery in emergencies.

New drugs may be developed to reverse the process of atherosclerosis, the formation of cholesterol-rich plaques on the interior walls of blood vessels that block the heart's supply of blood. University of Chicago scientists have used such drugs experimentally to shrink plaques in the blood vessels of monkeys. But heart transplants and artifical hearts may not fulfill the promise some experts once foresaw. They appear to have only limited usefulness, and then only in extreme cases.

If programs now under way to control high blood pressure succeed, strokes may be manageable by the end of the century. Strokes occur when the blood supply is cut off to parts of the brain by a dislodged clot or a bursting artery. Safer and more efficient drugs that reduce high blood pressure or prevent or dissolve clots may be developed.

Accidents. Among children and young adults, accidents are the leading cause of death. Of the quarter-million persons killed around the world in traffic accidents alone last year, 50,000, or one-fifth, were killed in the United States. Public health officials think educational and preventive measures similar to those employed against epidemic diseases could reduce the accident toll.

Viral diseases. Antibiotics already have revolutionized the battle against disease caused by bacteria. The development of chemicals to handle viruses, which are responsible for most disease, has been less successful. Still, by the end of the century, several new antiviral compounds probably will be used for the common cold, influenza, and herpes infections, which cause "cold sores" and may play a role in cervical cancer. There may be new and more effective antiviral vaccinations, too.

An inoculation against hepatitis, a widespread debilitating liver disease, is now being developed. It is likely to be perfected, perhaps well before the year 2000. Existing influenza vaccines, which confer poor protection and fast become useless against new strains of flu, may be succeeded by improved vaccines.

Today, vaccines are derived from the disease-causing viruses. Future vaccines may be entirely artificial. Some experts believe it will be possible to create vaccines that can immunize against a half-dozen diseases with a single injection. Such vaccines would be custom-tailored in the laboratory to compensate for the genetic vulnerabilities of individuals; viruses depend on the genetic material in cells to reproduce.

Birth defects. By 2000, recent emphasis on basic research in birth defects may have paid off. Simple screening methods for parents and "genetic counseling" could prevent the births, or permit the early identification, of babies with possible defects. Some defects will become treatable in the fetal stage. One possibility is "infecting" the fetus with a benign, man-made virus that delivers a missing gene to the cells.

Diabetes. Now thought to be the nation's third largest killer, diabetes may yield to new treatment by the end of the century. Some recent research suggests that a virus may cause the kind of diabetes that attacks youngsters. If so, it may be possible to screen genetically susceptible children and vaccinate them. The basic cause of diabetes, however, is still unknown. Diabetics are unable to properly metabolize the sugar they eat, leading to dangerously high blood-sugar levels, either because they do not produce enough sugar-regulating insulin or because of some other reason. Today, a common treatment is injection of insulin. In the future, pancreas transplants, or transplants of the specific pancreas cells responsible for sugar metabolism, could be more efficient. Current research also is aiming at the development of an artificial insulin-releasing pancreas.

Aging. In 2000, the average life will probably be only a few years longer than at present. But the biological mechanisms of aging will be better understood, and this will make geriatrics more useful as a medical specialty. In fact, geriatrics will be booming, with 28 million Americans over the age of sixty-five against 22 million today. As a major part of their job, geriatricians will use a wide variety of treatments and procedures, many of which now are available but underemployed, to delay the symptoms of senility.

Mental ailments. The split between those who believe that mental illness reflects chemical abnormalities in the brain and those who believe that mental illness is essentially of non-biochemical origin will still exist in 2000. Whatever the truth, many drugs today do alleviate the outward symptoms of mental illness to permit psychiatric treatment and encourage "normal" behavior. If mental illness is chemically based, then the illness itself might be treatable by drugs, too. On the other hand, some mental or emotional disorders may disappear simply because notions of what is normal and abnormal may change. Homosexuality and even certain psychoses have been accepted by some physicians and psychiatrists as natural and healthy, if not always socially acceptable.

Prosthetics. Researchers recently have reported successes with computer-controlled electronic devices, implanted in the brain, that transmit signals allowing totally blind persons to "see" Braille letters and read them. By 2000, advanced versions may be able to transmit videolike images of the outside world, perhaps from tiny camera transmitters in the blind person's eye sockets. And similar audio devices implanted in the inner ear could permit deaf persons to understand normal speech. An electrode that can detect human nerve impulses already has been developed. With refined engineering, the Harvard medical school scientists who designed it believe, it may be used to link severed nerves and reverse paralysis. It also would make possible direct brain control of electrically driven artificial arms, legs, and other prosthetic devices.

17

Breakthrough in Chemotherapy

After more than two decades of trial—and often error—drugs are starting to emerge as powerful front-line weapons against cancer. For the first time, doctors are talking of curing such once-hopeless malignancies as childhood leukemia and Hodgkin's disease with drugs. Already, more than half the children with a major form of leukemia treated experimentally with a regimen of drugs at a handful of outstanding cancer centers have passed the five-year mark alive and free of their disease. Many are well and disease-free after ten years. Some doctors call these children cured, although others hesitate to use that word, cautioning that they do not know for certain whether the cancer will ever recur. Even so, as new drug therapies are used more widely, many cancer experts predict, Americans should begin seeing, in the next two to three years (1978–1979), a dramatic change in the somber national death statistics on leukemia.

Emboldened by success, cancer researchers are starting to try drugs in the initial treatment of such widespread killers as cancer of the breast, colon, ovaries, and stomach. By employing the drugs at the right time before or immediately after surgery and radiation, the researchers hope to prevent the later recurrence of cancer. If this tactic works, it may soon be possible to reduce the extent of surgery.

There is a glimmer of hope, for example, that the use of drugs may enable surgeons, in many more cases of breast cancer than is possible now, to remove only the cancerous breast lump rather than perform a radical mastectomy, the removal of the entire breast and chest wall. "The whole pattern of using chemotherapy is changing," says Dr. Benjamin F. Byrd, Jr., a Vanderbilt University surgeon and past president of the American Cancer Society.

Researchers are cautious about just how far they may be able to go with the new drug attack on cancer. The whole field of chemotherapy has been marked by initial successes and high hopes followed by failures and deep disappointments. More than twenty-five years ago a wave of enthusiasm swept cancer laboratories when researchers, notably the late Dr. Sidney Farber of Children's Hospital in Boston, reported that such drugs as nitrogen mustard, a poison-gas derivative, had brought about complete remissions of leukemia in a few children. Unfortunately, the leukemia usually returned in a matter of months. It turned out that doctors had been able to give a few months more of life to children whose life expectancy was only four to six months when they were stricken.

But the dream of a chemical or a group of chemicals that could be wielded against cancer, just as antibiotics are used against bacterial disease, took hold. In the late 1950s the federal government began a program of testing literally hundreds of thousands of known chemicals for effectiveness in treating cancer. Despite several years of testing at a cost of hundreds of millions of dollars, this search failed to come up with the long-sought "magic bullet" against cancer.

Meanwhile, chemists began trying to tailor-make new chemicals to attack cancer cells. This long, tedious effort is starting to pay off. The armamentarium of anticancer drugs, which consisted of a mere half-dozen chemicals in the late 1950s, has gradually expanded to more than 50 drugs, more than half of which are being marketed commercially. The remainder are still classed as experimental.

More important, returns are beginning to come in on some once-daring experimental drug treatments launched in the mid-1960s with both newly developed and older chemicals. These returns have been slow for a good reason: Anticancer drugs are highly poisonous, and because of their danger they were largely limited to use in patients where the cancer was so far advanced anyway as to be beyond the powers of clinical surgery and radiation therapy. Thus, apparent failures were numerous and evident. For many years a cloud hung over chemotherapy, and in cases of apparent remission the reports far too often noted that the cancer had returned and the patient died.

At the same time, researchers were reluctant to claim success with drug therapy for fear their claims might be premature and might lead to abuse of chemotherapy. Instead, they waited until they had a significant number of patients alive and free of cancer for at least five years and in some cases ten years. It is these cases of five- and ten-year survivals that are now being reported.

One of the more dramatic drug successes has taken place in the treatment of childhood leukemia, the cancer of the blood-forming tissues that results in an abnormal production of immature white blood cells. Leukemia strikes an estimated 21,000 children a year. In 1976 it will cause about 15,000 deaths. Acute lymphocytic leukemia, which accounts for the vast majority of childhood leukemia cases, generally has been deemed incurable. In the mid-1960s, however, researchers at centers such as the National Cancer Institute in Bethesda, Maryland, began trying to overcome the major obstacle to the treatment of leukemia with drugs. This was the ability of the disease to develop a resistance to a drug after it was used for a few weeks or months.

The researchers devised a trick to zap the leukemia with one powerful drug followed by a different one. Combination chemotherapy apparently began to work. The number of children showing total remission of their leukemia began rising sharply. At the M. D. Anderson Hospital and Tumor Institute in Houston, Dr. Emil J. Freireich, a pioneer of combination chemotherapy, has reported that more than half the children treated five years ago or longer have stayed alive and free of any evidence of leukemia.

So far, the new therapy has failed to affect vital statistics. Figures for 1975 show that only 3 percent of acute-leukemia patients were surviving for as long as five years. Still, the mounting evidence that chemotherapy can be effective is encouraging its wider employment. Consequently, statistics should begin to show a sharp rise in the survival rate by 1978 or 1979.

A similar strategy is paying off in the treatment of advanced Hodgkin's disease, a leukemia-like cancer that affects the lymph system instead of the blood-forming system. Hodgkin's disease in its early stages can be cured with intense, deeply penetrating X rays, a treatment developed around 1970 at Stanford University. Unfortunately, many patients go undiagnosed or untreated until the disease has reached an advanced stage, and then radiation is far less effective. In the mid-1960s, some research groups began testing combinations of anticancer chemicals for advanced Hodgkin's disease. "At the time, we were frightened to death because of the experimental nature of the drugs," says Dr. Vincent T. DeVita, director of the Division of Cancer Treatment for the National Cancer Institute. He says there was considerable opposition to attempting to use combinations of poisonous drugs in cancer patients out of fear that such therapy would kill them.

But of 193 patients treated five years ago or more, 80 percent showed complete remission of their cancer in 1976. Of these patients, two-thirds are still alive and free of disease five to ten years after treatment. "Of all the people who walk in the door, 70 percent can be cured," Dr. DeVita says. Such results have encouraged cancer researchers to begin to experiment with chemotherapy in other difficult cancers. Though the results so far are promising, the experimenters are cautious in evaluating them.

A particularly virulent form of lung cancer, oat-cell carcinoma, accounts for about one-sixth of 93,000 cases of lung cancer diagnosed each year. Of the victims of oat-cell carcinoma, 80 percent are dead within one year after diagnosis.

Only 5 percent live for five years. At the National Cancer Institute, researchers have begun to combine intensive radiation therapy with three powerful drugs: cytoxan, adriamycin, and vincristine. Seventeen of the first twenty-two patients thus treated were alive and disease-free four to fourteen months after treatment. The disease renewed itself in four of the twenty-two. One patient died, partly because of complications arising from the treatment itself. To Dr. DeVita, the figures suggest that "we're at the point where we were with acute leukemia a decade ago."

At the University of California in Los Angeles, researchers are tackling some rare but lethal bone and soft-tissue cancers, the sarcomas, afflicting 2,000 to 3,000 children each year. Amputation has been the usual answer for bone sarcoma, which usually afflicts a limb. But even after amputation, the cancer recurs in a large number of cases because the cancerous cells already have spread.

The UCLA researchers have developed a therapeutic procedure that seeks to avoid amputation. It begins with the administering of adriamycin, one of the newer anticancer drugs, also used in cases of oat-cell carcinoma. X rays are employed in an attempt to destroy the existing bone tumor. The diseased part of the bone is next removed surgically and replaced with a graft. Then comes a daring drug treatment pioneered by Dr. Isaac Djerassi, of Darby, Pennsylvania. Doses of an older anticancer drug, methotrexate, are given in quantities that ordinarily would be deadly. But before the patient dies—and, it is hoped, after the drug has eliminated any remaining tumor cells—an antidote is administered. By early 1976, the UCLA researchers had treated fifteen patients in this manner. All were alive, some having survived for as long as eighteen months. And none had recurrences of their sarcoma.

Sarcomas and some other kinds of cancers that have been prime targets of the new chemotherapies are among the less common cancers. Even if 15,000 lives a year could be saved with the procedures now being proved effective, Dr. DeVita observes, "this number can easily be viewed as unimpressive when mingled with a total of 350,000 cancer deaths each year." But researchers now are preparing to throw chemicals into the battle against more common cancers, such as those of the breast and colon. This offers a potential for saving 50,000 to 100,000 lives a year, Dr. DeVita says.

The big barrier to cures in these cases never has been removal of the primary tumor. Surgery or radiation can almost always eliminate the main tumor. But by the time of diagnosis, the tumor often has released its lethal microscopic clumps of cells into the bloodstream or lymph stream. These metastases have lodged in other parts of the body well beyond the reach of the knife, and eventually they trigger the spread of the cancer, and death. Because anticancer chemicals can operate anywhere in the body, they stand a chance of eliminating the metastases.

Initial successes with radiotherapy and chemotherapy suggest a program for possible effective treatment of breast cancer. First, surgery to remove the tumor, leaving the breast intact, followed by radiation to wipe out the unexcised remnants of the tumor. Then, if a biopsy shows that the cancer has spread through the lymph nodes, a round of drug treatments. As it is now, surgeons often remove the entire breast in an often-unsuccessful attempt to cut off the cancer before it spreads.

Summary

Turn to any one of dozens of how-to books and brochures dealing with the building and preservation of personal fortunes, and you probably will find that it ignores the single most important asset the family breadwinner has: his or her health. Very few people, indeed, hold financial assets capable of yielding an income of $6,000, the average American's personal income in 1975.

Most adult Americans are aware of the economic value of their health, and so are their life insurance companies, even if economists and the writers of get-rich tomes are not. It is to the future of health—its fundamental sustenance in the form of food and its maintenance by medical and nonmedical measures—that the foregoing section addresses itself.

The prospect for health is far from utopian. A "grim progression [in population growth] threatens to overcrowd the globe and strain its ability to feed, clothe, and shelter its inhabitants." By the year 2000, only the United States and Canada may be exporting grain. The leaders of these nations may be forced to allocate foodstuffs selectively, in effect dooming to starvation unlucky or powerless groups in the world's population. The possibility has emerged that the relatively

115

high level of productivity in world agriculture in recent decades has been the happy consequence of a climatic fluke. The world may undergo decades of drought and other unfavorable cyclical changes in climate.

If in many nations political and institutional flaws have hindered greater agricultural productivity, as a group of United Nations experts and others recently have suggested, these man-made impediments to enriching the larder will not readily disappear. The "green revolution" is neither so green nor so revolutionary as it once appeared to be.

In medicine, scientific and technological breakthroughs have produced striking advances in the treatment of many diseases. The professional dedication of many medical and other scientific researchers has won these gains. But doctors and other professionals are delivering a sober message. Overall, not even the most dramatic conquests of disease are going to extend average life expectancies by more than a modest span.

Some people are heeding the message. In their diets and ways of life, they are trying to reduce workaday stress, avoid overeating, and conserve what they increasingly seem to perceive as finite sources of food and energy.

All of this is likely to have diverse and difficult-to-predict effects on the management of American business. Given the spiraling increase in costs of medical care, one strong implication is that employers will begin to take a more active interest in health maintenance and other forms of preventive medicine for their employees. Through taxes or insurance programs, corporations already are financing a huge portion of the nation's medical bill, and it clearly is in the corporate interest to make sure that the money is efficiently spent.

The federal government and corporate managers themselves have taken an intense interest in the establishment and financing of pension and profit-sharing plans adequate to provide a comfortable living for retired employees. It is not difficult to imagine that, as an extension of this interest, the government and business will step up their efforts toward maintaining the health of employees.

In agriculture, the bleak outlook for the world in general

can only enhance the already critical role of large corporate American food producers. Most agricultural experts would concede the superb efficiency that private corporate enterprise has brought to agricultural production in America. If their political or institutional structure prevents many other nations from achieving similar efficiency, American food and agricultural machinery producers still are likely to find ready markets abroad for their expertise and for their products.

But problems of population growth and hunger abroad can only hinder the expansion of world trade. American and multinational corporations are likely to find it an increasingly risky business. The political and economic instability of nations suffering from these problems will make it difficult to provide the sound financing demanded by expanding world trade. It will require a great deal of corporate ingenuity and risk-taking to cope with some of the constraints on trade, and a sophisticated understanding of the problems by government; and sadly, even this may not be sufficient.

Perhaps this is too gloomy a picture. An occasional success story abroad does suggest that poor nations can and will cope with some of their fundamental deficiencies. As the Philippine experience in the "green revolution" shows, progress can be very slow, but it nonetheless remains progress. Egypt's energetic program to reduce its population growth provides another example of measurable, if painfully slow, improvement. International cooperation in aid and trade agreements holds at least the possibility of instigating some important reforms and improvements elsewhere in the world. American and multinational corporations may become important beneficiaries of any increase in world income.

III
MATERIALS MANAGEMENT
Energy, Housing, and Transportation

18

Energy in 2000

The primary sources of energy today are coal, oil, and natural gas. In the year 2000, energy experts generally agree, the chief sources of energy will still be coal, oil, and natural gas. This may suggest that little has changed since 1966, when the *Wall Street Journal* reported that the earth still held enough fossil fuels to keep homes warm and factories humming for centuries. But a lot has changed. In 1966, nuclear power was expected to hold a commanding position among energy sources in 2000. The combination of near-limitless supplies of nuclear power and vast resources of fossil fuels was expected to produce abundant and cheap energy even though consumption would triple by 2000.

Nuclear power today faces an uncertain future. Much else has changed since the rosy forecasts of a decade earlier. The environmental movement and a few Arab sheikhs have rewritten the world's energy texts. Thanks to the oil cartel and the 1973–1974 Arab oil embargo, petroleum prices have quadrupled. American oil output has peaked, and it now is declining. Energy, then, may not be so abundant in 2000. Certainly it will not be cheap. And so it will be used in lesser amounts than prophets in 1966 predicted. But the cost, rather than the availability, will constrain the use of energy. "There won't be a worldwide energy shortage this century," says John H. Lichtblau, executive director of the Petroleum Industry Research Foundation.

In short, the decades-long era of cheap energy has ended.

The economic repercussions have had a sharp impact on the lifestyles and living standards of people around the world, and for years to come the repercussions will continue. By choking off their oil, as they did during the winter of 1973–74, Mideast producers demonstrated their ability to humble the world's mightiest nations. And oil as a political weapon creates the prospect that some future wars may be fought over it.

Ten years ago, it was inconceivable that American motorists would wait in gasoline lines because of an oil embargo. At the time, the United States was self-sufficient in energy. It was the world's leading oil producer, and it had enough coal to last 300 to 400 years or more. In a pinch, like the Suez crisis in 1957, it could rescue European nations by sending them the oil they lacked.

The United States still has lots of coal, which may be its energy salvation. But it is no longer self-sufficient in energy. The Soviet Union has overtaken it in oil output, and America is becoming increasingly dependent on foreign oil. Thus the implications of a future embargo are growing more serious.

Today, nearly 40 percent of the oil consumed in the United States is imported as crude oil or as refined products. "At anticipated production and consumption rates, we probably will be importing half the oil we consume by the end of the decade," says Howard W. Blauvelt, chairman of Continental Oil Company.

Petroleum production in the United States, now 8.1 million barrels a day, has fallen since 1970, when it peaked at 9.6 million barrels a day. By 1978, domestic oil output probably will level as new supplies flow from the North Slope of Alaska. The leveling, however, is expected to be only temporary. Unless new fields of the magnitude of the North Slope are found—in Alaska, offshore, or in the lower forty-eight states—output will fall again. Even if these big new fields are found, energy analysts say, the rise in consumption from the United States' modest population growth alone will keep widening the gap between domestic oil supplies and demand. Most of the oil needed to fill that gap will have to come from Mideast fields. Yet, political and economic obstacles aside, will there be enough of this oil to meet American needs as well as those of other oil-importing nations? Not indefinitely. It is true that big new oil producers are emerging, notably Mexico and China. It is possible that some giant new reservoirs, like the North Sea fields, will produce a lot of oil before 2000. This new flow could be large enough to break the price of oil, if not the structure of the cartel. Even so, oil economists expect that world consumption will exceed the rate at which new reserves of oil are added. They doubt that anything like the vast reservoirs in the Mideast will be found anywhere else. "We thus have entered an era during which we will be continually drawing down reserves of oil and gas," says Clifton C. Garvin, Jr., chairman of Exxon Corporation.

Many oil analysts agree with studies by Texaco Inc. that suggest the world's output and reserves of oil will start their final long decline around 1990. "Unlike the present situation," says Maurice F. Granville, Texaco chairman, "we will then be competing for world oil in a market where supplies are becoming increasingly scarce."

The petroleum era appears likely to last until 2020 or beyond. Until then, the Petroleum Industry Research Foundation's Lichtblau thinks, "oil will still be widely used for transportation, with other energy needs met by other sources."

In 1966, it seemed easy to predict that those "other sources" mainly meant nuclear energy. The *Wall Street Journal* reported forecasts that there would be "almost limitless supplies of power from nuclear plants, expected eventually to be the cheapest source of energy almost everywhere on the globe." It already has become clear, however, that nuclear power is no panacea. In fact, some observers consider it a sick industry. Costs are escalating. Environmentalists are attacking it on a broad front. Uranium shortages loom, and some people think the world will run out of uranium before it runs out of oil.

The highly touted "breeder" reactors that would create plutonium for use from their own spent fuel are highly expensive and may never prove economic. There is vociferous and growing opposition to the widespread use of plutonium fuel because of numerous health and safety hazards. Without breeder reactors, nuclear power's future is probably limited. Nevertheless, it will be important. The United States now has fifty-eight conventional uranium reactors in operation. The nuclear power industry expects the number to exceed 200 by 1985. By the end of the century, 800 are likely to be needed. Whether they will be running is conjectural. One of the more optimistic projections for nuclear power comes from the Bureau of Mines. In a recent series of energy forecasts, the bureau predicted that nuclear power will supply a little more than 28 percent of the nation's energy by 2000, up from less than 2 percent today. The forecast assumes, however, that breeder reactors will operate commercially between 1985 and 2000. And it is unclear that they will do so.

David E. Lilienthal, who had headed the Tennessee Valley Authority and became the first chairman of the Atomic Energy Commission, flatly says that "the atom is here to stay." And according to William W. Havens, Jr., professor of physics at Columbia University, nuclear power offers "the cleanest and environmentally most satisfying solution" to energy problems. But even Professor Havens concedes that the "uncertainties" surrounding nuclear power are more critical than the projections of its possible use. The future of nuclear fusion, he says, is even more speculative.

Fusion involves the merger, rather than the splitting, of atoms to produce energy. In 1966, it was hailed as the ultimate energy source, largely because the hydrogen it would use as fuel is so abundant. Still, nobody knows how to build a fusion reactor. In theory it could be built, and it would work, but its theory has never been proved in practice.

An alternative to hydrogen fusion is its burning as a fuel. Hydrogen already is being extracted from oil and natural gas for certain manufacturing and refining processes. Every molecule of water contains hydrogen. It can be liberated by an electrical process. It is nonpolluting, releasing only water when burned. But processing it is so costly that using it for fuel would require, in effect, entirely retooling the nation's energy system. Energy students think it will have no important role as a fuel until long after 2000.

One renewable source of energy is available: the sun. Nuclear physicists like Professor Havens and environmentalists like Washington University's Barry Commoner agree on its promise for supplementing and eventually supplanting fossil fuels. By restoring the backyard clothesline, any homeowner even now can substitute solar energy for some fossil-fuel energy at a trivial capital cost. And on the premise that any building under the sun is "essentially a solar collector," Walter S. White, an architect in Colorado Springs, has long designed homes that make use of sunlight. He has patented a "solar heat exchanger window-wall" assembly that he says will heat and cool an entire building. He proposes the construction of central solar power plants to provide the energy needed for new energy-sufficient communities limited to 7,000 or 7,500 residents.

The sun, sadly, bestows its blessings unevenly. To supply much power, solar collectors would have to cover vast acreages in the southwestern United States. Equipping homes with solar heating and cooling devices is very costly. The fabrication of solar devices itself requires a great deal of expensive energy. Futurists generally doubt that anybody now living will ever live in a solar-powered, cheap-energy utopia. Shell Oil Company goes as far as anyone else in projecting the role of solar power. A study by Shell, which owns an interest in a Delaware-based solar energy concern, suggests that by 2000 "all forms of solar energy could reasonably be expected to supply as much as 15 percent of total U.S. demand."

A variety of other seemingly unlikely sources may provide smaller proportions of the nation's energy. Burning trash may power some generators. The University of Rochester in New York has launched an ambitious industry-financed undertaking to use the laser in the controlled fusion of hydrogen nuclei, an idea that boasts some theoretical superiority to other fusion proposals. But this program, experts concede, is more than three decades away from producing "clean, virtually limitless power"—if it ever does so.

Schemes have been designed to harness the power of ocean tides and of heat in the ocean and deep within the earth. Geothermal energy—steam—already is produced from relatively shallow wells drilled much like oil wells. Processes, costly ones, are available to produce oil and gas from the nation's abundant oil-shale and coal reserves.

TRW Inc., the electronics conglomerate, has done special studies and development work for government agencies in solar energy, geothermal sources, oil-shale potential, coal gasification, and large-scale energy storage batteries. Yet John S. Foster, Jr., general manager of TRW's energy systems group, says that "in 2000, we are still going to be using oil, gas, and coal and still running nuclear plants." This is so partly because even any dramatic energy discoveries or breakthroughs will require years to become commercially important. The Energy Research and Development Administration (ERDA) notes that historically it has taken some sixty years from the point at which a transition to a new energy source was first discernible until that source reached its peak use and began to decline. Domestic supplies of oil and gas appear to have reached their peak, ERDA concludes, and "it is essential, therefore, to plan now for the transition from oil and gas to new sources to supply the next energy cycle."

Actually, an old source—coal—will supply the next energy cycle. The United States is richly endowed with it, holding at least one quarter of the world's reserves, more than enough to offset any decline in oil and gas output. But coal will not be cheap. Environmental constraints, a shortage of skilled manpower to exploit all the mines that will be needed, and enormous capital requirements will make it dear. Even so, output by 2000 may double and possibly triple 1975's record 640 million tons. Coal may supply more than 25 percent of total energy demand—as much as, or more than, nuclear power will supply in 2000.

Rising petroleum prices have sharply curtailed growth projections in total energy demand. Most estimates now put the rate of growth in demand in the United States at less than 3 percent a year for the rest of the twentieth century, compared with 4 percent to 5 percent a year in the period before the 1973–1974 oil embargo. Foster of TRW thus concludes: "The biggest revolution in energy will be in the business of energy consumption."

19

Solar Power

American energy researchers are drawing up elaborate and costly plans for the home and factory of the future to plug into the power of the sun. The aim is to convert the sun's limitless energy into electricity on a massive scale. Construction has begun in Albuquerque on a pioneering project. Three hundred and twenty huge mirrors on the ground will reflect sunlight onto a boiler atop a 200-foot concrete tower. Water in the boiler will become steam. Eventually the steam could be used to produce electricity. Testing of the solar tower is to begin in 1977 at the Energy Research and Development Administration's Sandia Laboratories in New Mexico. ERDA plans to complete another solar tower in 1980; it will produce 10,000 kilowatts of electricity, enough to serve a town of about 10,000 people. This project would be the nation's solar electric pilot plant.

The technology to build and operate the plant exists. "We know it will make electricity," says George Kaplan, an ERDA official. "There isn't any high technology here. A mirror is a mirror."

Solar power clearly has dazzling promise. Its advocates see it as a means of avoiding energy shortages that threaten as the earth's oil and natural gas supplies dwindle and as coal and nuclear power encounter increased public concern over pollution and safety. But to more pragmatic energy planners, the dazzle is distant. The first commercial-size generating plant seems out of reach before 1990. And not until the turn of the century is the new power source expected to be commonplace. Even including solar energy other than solar electricity, ERDA officials forecast that sun power will supply only 7 percent of the nation's energy by the end of this century, though a more optimistic nongovernmental study puts the potential at 15 percent.

The capital cost of commercial solar power will be high, partly because it will require complex storage systems to supply power on overcast days. Thus electricity produced by solar power will be costly. "The technology is already here, but solar [power] isn't yet economically competitive with other energy forms," says Henry H. Marvin, director of ERDA's solar division. ERDA economist Paul Maycock calculates that a solar power station today using a reflecting tower could cost $7,500 per kilowatt of generating capacity to build, five times the cost at which it would be competitive with fossil-fueled plants of intermediate size.

At the Sandia Laboratories, operated for ERDA by Western Electric Company, the cost problems are already visible. They arise in part from the amount of land required by a solar tower facility. The 1977 test alone will require about 100 acres, says Arthur J. Clark, Jr., project manager. About 40 acres are needed just for the 320 twenty-foot-square mirrors that will reflect the sun's rays on the tower. The remaining sixty acres will contain the reflection zone, the tower, and various test buildings.

The mirrors are especially costly. Each is mounted on a motor-driven device that tracks the sun across the sky. Future solar tower plants may require 20,000 or more of these heliostats. Their cost is critical to the economic feasibility of such plants. Piet Bos, solar program manager for the Electric Power Research Institute, thinks that if mass production could bring their cost to $7 per square foot of mirror area, the plant could compete. The price now would be three or four times that figure.

ERDA's contractors, Martin Marietta Corporation, McDonnell Douglas Corporation, and Honeywell Inc., are developing various experimental energy-storage systems for the 10,000 kilowatt pilot plant. Storage devices would hold enough energy in the form of heat to maintain the plant's electrical output for four to six hours. But any larger storage capacity would hike the system's cost above competitive levels, according to ERDA officials.

So it is anticipated that solar electric plants in the foreseeable future mainly will supply power in the sunny Southwest, and then only as a supplement to more conventional sources. The Southwest plants are likely to be of intermediate size, each generating between 50,000 and 150,000 kilowatts, compared to the 1-million-kilowatt coal-fired and nuclear plants that utilities now are building.

There is some disagreement over the significance of solar electricity costs, however. Floyd Blake, an executive of Martin Marietta, thinks that current economic obstacles result from a "natural cycle" and that "cost reduction is the last stage of any new development. The first computers," he observes, "weren't cost-effective." Solar electric plants will become economically competitive with nuclear plants and some fossil-fuel plants, he believes, sometime between 1990 and 1995. Some critics, too, complain that the government and industry have failed to pursue solar electricity as energetically as they should. In *The Poverty of Power*, environmentalist Barry Commoner charged that the government has dismissed the sun's power potential as "only a faint distant hope." Commoner believes it could replace most and perhaps all of the sources now utilizing conventional fuels.

That complaint aside, ERDA still is spending two-thirds of its solar energy dollars on electricity generation, the remaining one-third on heating and cooling via rooftop heat-collecting. "Solar electricity has the most eventual impact, the highest payoff," says James Mitchell, the White House's chief energy-budget officer. And the solar tower approach is only one ERDA-backed project to generate electricity from sunlight. Another major effort is in solar cells that convert sunlight directly into electricity without towers or mirrors. Solar cells can do this because sunlight activates electrons in a disk of light-sensitive material. Joseph Lindmayer, president of Solarex Corporation, Rockville, Maryland, thinks that solar cells by 1985 will be commercially available for installation atop buildings. Others envision the cells in utility generating stations or in orbiting satellites that would beam power to ground receivers even through cloud cover.

Solar cells, first developed for space exploration, already have small-scale applications in remote localities. They power some radio equipment and energize lights on buoys. In a Forest Service restroom in Montana, solar cells supply electric current. But their high cost is holding back their commercial use. ERDA calculates the average cost of a cell capable of generating one watt at $20. At 50 cents, officials say, solar-cell electricity might be feasible. The government aims at getting the cost down to that level by 1985.

At the present capital cost of $20 a cell, it thus would cost a utility $20,000 to build a solar cell plant with generating capacity of one kilowatt. Maycock, the ERDA economist, calculates that storage capability of three to six hours of output would raise the cost to $40,000 or $50,000 per kilowatt. The cost of such a system somehow would have to tumble all the way to $1,000 or $1,100 a kilowatt, in today's dollars, to make it economically feasible.

Much of the cost of solar-cell electricity lies in the manufacture of the cell. Most solar cells are made from silicon, the second most abundant element on earth, usually found in a compound form, as in sand; refining silicon to the necessary purity in a single-crystal form is extremely costly. Efforts are being made to shrink the cost. Mobil Tyco Solar Energy Corporation, a joint venture of Mobil Oil Corporation and Tyco Laboratories Inc., is working on reducing the cost by speeding the processing of silicon. Other companies are experimenting with cell materials that might be produced less expensively than silicon. Cadmium sulfide and gallium arsenide are possibilities. At Sandia, researchers are taking still another approach. They are using optical lenses to concentrate sunlight on solar cells to increase their electrical output. The use of the lenses may produce a given wattage with fewer cells. One lens atop a laboratory building at Sandia has increased the output of a solar cell from one-fifth of a watt to ten watts. In the summer of 1976, Sandia was placing in operation a system of 150 lenses and 150 solar cells expected to produce one kilowatt.

Researchers are trying still other ways to turn sun power into electricity. They have built a complete solar energy system that actually produces electricity on a test scale. What was a parking lot in 1975 now is covered with a score of 9-by-12-foot aluminum reflectors. They track the sun and reflect its rays to a thin tube of a chemical called toluene, an ingredient of TNT. The vapor of the heated toluene drives a small turbine. This system is designed also to make use of the heat normally wasted. Engineers intend to use the electricity for lighting a nearby building and to channel otherwise unused heat into the building for its heating and air conditioning system.

Designs like this eventually may "provide all the energy needed by small subdivisions, apartment buildings, or shopping centers," Sandia researcher James A. Leonard says. ERDA plans to determine the economics of such a design in 1979 or 1980 with a pilot plant capable of serving twenty houses or a twenty-unit apartment building.

Other research work at Sandia is devoted to the generation of power from wind (actually a form of solar energy, because winds are created by the sun's unequal heating of the atmosphere) and from ocean currents (which are influenced by the sun's unequal warming of seawater). By 2020, if not before, ERDA officials think, these or other forms of solar energy may be inexpensive enough to supply 15 percent of the nation's electrical output.

20
Happy Tinkerers

So far as Robert Reines is concerned, Arab countries can turn off the oil tomorrow and electricity costs can go through the roof. He is insulated from all that. He lives in Tijeras, New Mexico, in an igloolike white dome that gets its heat from the sun and its electricity from the wind. The dome home is on a hillside some twenty miles from Albuquerque. At night, the inside lights shining through the dome's portholes conjure up a scene from an H. G. Wells novel.

Reines sees himself as a pioneer of an age when entire communities will be self-sufficient in energy. "I have freedom because I have all the energy I need," he says with a bristling fervor, "and that's real freedom."

Of course, Reines still drives a conventional gasoline-powered automobile. And New Mexico's winters, less severe than those of some other places, make it possible for him to keep his home warm. He has lived comfortably for three winters in his energy-independent house, however, even when outside temperatures have fallen below freezing.

While the government's Project Independence remains largely a dream, their own energy independence is becoming a reality for a small group of architects, engineers, and plain happy tinkerers. Their homes rely on a variety of ingenious methods to produce and store energy. All are equipped with devices to collect solar energy, and some have windmill generators for electricity. The homes store their heat in large water tanks, in rocks under floors, or in concrete walls. And the homes are tightly insulated in some unusual ways.

In Guilford, Connecticut, Everett Barber has built a $50,000 home equipped with a huge south-facing picture window, several tons of rock under his floor, rooftop solar panels, and a windmill. In Beallsville, Ohio, Warren Stetzel has been digging a large excavation for an underground house to be insulated by the earth. At McGill University in Montreal and at the University of Minnesota in Minneapolis, architecture students have developed energy-independent houses. In Allentown, the Pennsylvania Power and Light Company has spent $140,000 on a house to demonstrate that a combination of gadgetry can cut heating and cooling bills strikingly.

It is noteworthy that these efforts largely are privately financed. Despite Washington's ambitious program for energy independence, focusing on such things as nuclear power and coal research, little research money is trickling down to energy conservation at the family level. "We tried to get the National Science Foundation to grant us $30,000 to develop a simple heat storage system, but we were turned down cold," says Steve Baer, an energy researcher and the owner of a solar house in Albuquerque. "There hasn't been any government money put into a project that would tell a person how to build something in his own backyard." In Butler, Pennsylvania, architect Richard Rittleman has a similar complaint. He has designed an advanced energy-saving home for a woman who wants to use the building to train architecture and engineering students. "We tried to get government research funding, but none was forthcoming, so the project has been shelved for the moment," he says.

There is a ray of hope. Late in 1974, the Solar Heating and Cooling Demonstration Act, under which the Housing and Urban Development Department and the National Aeronautics and Space Administration could each spend $5 million on research, was enacted. From HUD's share, some $98,000 is going to the research arm of the American Institute of Architects, which has spread the money among ten design firms and architecture schools for research on energy-saving equipment and homes.

In 1975, according to a University of Colorado survey, there were nearly 200 solar-heated houses built, under construction, or planned in the United States. To equip these and future houses, more than 100 solar-equipment makers have gone into business, many of them small, backyard concerns. But the solar-power market, according to a study by Arthur D. Little and Company, could reach $1.3 billion by 1985 "if industry, with effective government support, moves ahead promptly to introduce solar hardware into the marketplace."

Now this hardware is high priced. It is largely handmade from expensive materials such as copper, and large amounts usually are needed. A commonly used rooftop solar panel is a glass-covered aluminum or steel tray in which antifreeze, water, or air is heated as it moves through blackened copper tubing. In many parts of the United States, such heat collectors must cover at least 50 percent of the roof surface to provide about 80 percent of a house's central heating.

Fred Dubin, of the New York engineering firm of Dubin-Mindell-Bloome Associates, designers of a number of solar buildings, says that even at today's high fuel prices, in most areas of the country it can take fifteen to twenty years to recover an investment in solar-heating equipment. Everett Barber, who teaches at Yale University and in his spare time runs a small company that makes solar collectors, says that "at present, solar power is still mainly for the rich." Barber should know. He struggled to keep down the cost on the small energy-saving home he built in Guilford.

The center of the two-story house's heating system is a massive, 2,000 gallon water tank, warmed by antifreeze that is heated by rooftop solar collectors. Surrounding the warm sides of the tank is a sheath of corrugated aluminum. Air is drawn through channels in the metal and is then blown by a fan over tons of crushed rock under the ground floor. The rock retains heat but lets it gradually rise up through the floor. Warm air also is circulated by the fan through ducts leading to three upstairs bedrooms.

What Barber calls low-level heat helps. This is heat generated by people in the house, heat from cooking, and heat from the morning sunlight that pours into the house from its large picture window and two sliding glass doors. This heat rises to the top of the house, where it is drawn down by the fan through a central duct to the rock. Solar panes, and his rock system, provide Barber with 80 percent of his central heating. The rest comes from a wood-burning fireplace.

A system like this one requires a tightly insulated house. Barber's is built of cinder blocks sprayed with a three-inch coat of polyurethane to prevent inside heat from escaping. This gives the exterior a stucco appearance. Little heat in the house is wasted. Solar panels supply hot air for the clothes dryer. Hot water used for washing is preheated by the panels and then "topped up" by heat from electricity provided by the wind generator. The wood fireplace helps heat the water storage tank. The fireplace uses cold air vented in from the exterior for combustion, conserving warm interior air.

But Barber ran into a host of problems. The town balked at giving him permission to erect a 60-foot tower for his $2,500 windmill. He ran out of storage space for his 11-foot water tank; it stands obtrusively in the corner of his living room. He insists that his wife does not mind it. "We've made it a design element of the house," he says. "It's like a Grecian urn." But the elephantine urn is taking up a considerable chunk of living space.

And there is the cost. Barber thought that a $50,000 mortgage would allow him to build a sizable house. But the cost of his energy system kept growing, to $13,000, and the house got smaller.

Designers around the country are trying to bring down such costs. One novel approach is that of a group of architects and engineers in Harrisville, New Hampshire, who formed Total Environmental Action. The organization has designed a house for a family in Manchester using a concrete wall to collect and store solar heat.

The south wall is 12-inch-thick blackened concrete

covered with two layers of fibrous glass. The concrete stores heat for circulation through interior ducts. At night, tiny beads of plastic foam, automatically blown into a 3-inch space between the glass sheets, insulate the concrete to reduce heat loss. In the morning, the beads are sucked out of the space to permit sunlight to strike the concrete.

Reines's system in New Mexico is equally ingenious. His steel dome, 30 feet in diameter, is made up of about ninety pieces. They could be bolted together by four people in about twelve hours. The inside of the dome is sprayed with polyurethane. Heat comes from a series of solar panels arrayed on the hillside above the dome (although, on a new dome home Reines is planning, the panels are built into the roof). The panels heat antifreeze, which in turn flows down to heat a huge tank supplying water for the dome's baseboard heating system. Electricity comes from thirty-year-old windmills that Reines found abandoned on nearby farms and installed atop towers on his thirty acres. Without free windmills, Reines doubts that wind-generated electricity would be feasible for a single family.

Dome development cost Reines, a former Air Force engineer, some $80,000, of which about $50,000 came from a research foundation. No new outside financing is in sight, however.

His energy-saving existence is a frugal one. Because of the limited amount of electricity he gets from his windmills, he has few appliances, and he does all his cooking in an energy-saving microwave oven. But Reines, bearded and feisty, growls, "I have all the energy I need. A dishwasher isn't freedom."

In Beallsville, Ohio, Warren Stetzel takes the view that energy frugality "doesn't mean the end of civilization." He is building a house that, he says, will allow all the usual creature comforts. Energy will come from solar and wind systems supplemented by utility-company power. But the most unusual thing about this house is that it is being built underground of concrete poured in a hole in a hillside on 850 acres that Stetzel and a group of friends bought four years ago to save from strip mining. The house will be insulated largely by the hillside's 3½ feet of sod, perhaps the oldest insulating material known.

By contrast, up-to-date technology is being used by Pennsylvania Power and Light Company to show how power bills can be drastically cut. The utility has spent $50,000 on an experimental house (plus $90,000 on research) that is being heated and cooled for about $200 a year in electricity, compared with about $500 for a conventional house of the same size.

The 1,700-square-foot house, just outside Allentown, was occupied for a year by company employee Kenneth Borger and his family. They put up with a basement crammed with the pipes and gadgetry that make up the heating and cooling system. It consists of two main elements: solar panels and heat pumps. The pump absorbs heat from outside air to warm the inside air. In summer it reverses itself and becomes an air conditioner. Its efficiency lies in its ability, varying with the outdoor temperature, to extract three times as much heat energy from the outside air as the electrical energy consumed by the pump.

An insulated water tank in the basement stores the heat produced by the outside heat pump and by the solar panels that form a screen outside the house. The tank also stores excess heat from such sources as the clothes dryer and waste water. Heated water from the tank is then used in an inside pump for central heating.

Bob Romanchek, the utility's research director, says, "We can bring the heating costs below $200 a year."

21

Building Conservation into Products

You've heard the old canard: The big light-bulb manufacturers really know how to make a bulb that would last almost forever, but they are carefully keeping it off the market. And if a buyer occasionally does get a long-lasting bulb, one story goes, it is only because a company inspector happened to blink. In fact, the big manufacturers appear innocent of any such conspiracy. But now a two-man company has come along with a new kind of bulb said to last for years, perhaps even decades, and to emit the same amount of light as a conventional bulb while using only one-fourth to one-third the electricity.

The creator is a California inventor named Donald Hollister. His product has no filaments to burn out. It works something like a fluorescent light but looks like a standard bulb and screws into a standard socket. Though the new bulb probably will cost $10 when it is first marketed, its savings on electricity promise to offset the stiff initial cost. Hollister hopes his bulb will replace the incandescent lamp invented nearly a century ago by Thomas Edison. What is more, the Energy Research and Development Administration has some faith in Hollister. It has awarded his Lighting Technology Corporation of Fullerton, California, a $310,000 one-year contract to perfect the bulb, which was ballyhooed at a press conference in March 1976 in Washington. "It works," an ERDA lighting expert says. "The bulb needs to be made more sophisticated, but indications are that it can be commercially feasible."

The Hollister light bulb's inventor has a background in physics and has worked on lighting systems for various companies. He first came up with the theory of the better bulb in 1965 and three years later described it to the world in a paper given at a scientific symposium at Gatlinburg, Tennessee. Nobody beat a path to his door. "The reaction was no particular reaction at all," he says, but then the energy crunch had not yet arrived.

During the 1973–1974 oil embargo, Hollister approached some lighting companies but was rebuffed by what he calls the NIH Factor. It means, Not Invented Here. "It is difficult to bring technology into a company from outside the organization because of the NIH Factor," he says. In 1975, however Hollister interested ERDA in his bulb and got a contract to develop it.

Instead of hot filaments, the Hollister bulb uses a coil of cool wire that generates a magnetic field inside the bulb. This field induces currents that stimulate mercury vapor in the bulb to produce light. While the principles are similar to those employed in fluorescent lighting, the Hollister bulb would work where any conventional one does. It uses about 30 percent as much electricity as an equivalent incandescent bulb, ERDA says, and because it has no filaments to burn out, it can last a long time. Just how long has not been determined.

The light-bulb project is but one sample of efforts of ERDA, one of two agencies created by Congress in 1975 to replace the old Atomic Energy Commission. ERDA's professed goal is to improve existing technology so as to save energy. The agency is promoting a variety of projects, including research and development to improve the life of batteries for electric cars; to heat a house in winter by extracting heat from water, turning the water to ice, and cooling the house in summer by melting the ice; to use waste heat from the exhaust of large trucks to help power them; and to perfect an automatic valve for old radiators that serves, like a thermostat on modern heaters, to conserve heat.

Austin Heller, assistant administrator for energy conservation research, says the effort is aimed at "building or locking conservation into products."

An ERDA-sponsored Annual Cycle Energy System (ACES) would save energy in heating and cooling houses. ERDA officials say the system could halve the energy consumed in space heating and cooling in parts of the United States where there is a near-balance between annual heating and cooling requirements—generally the area as far north as Minneapolis and as far south as Atlanta. ACES would employ a heat pump—a heat-transfer device already in use—and a water-ice storage system in development at ERDA's Oak Ridge, Tennessee, laboratory. A house to test the technology is under construction at the University of Tennessee. The heart of ACES would be a 7½-foot insulated tank containing some 3,000 cubic feet of water. The tank would occupy about one-third of the house basement, or it would be installed beneath the basement.

In winter, the heat pump would draw warmth from the water for heating. "All water has some heat in it," David Pellish, an ERDA buildings technologist, observes. The heat would circulate through the house by forced air or some other system. Over several months, removal of the heat from the water would turn the water into ice. In the summer, the ice would be used to chill air that would be blown through the house. As the ice melted, it would become water that would store heat for winter use.

Such a system could save hundreds of dollars a year in heating and cooling an average house, ERDA officials claim. Of course there is a catch. ACES would cost an estimated $2,000 more to buy and install than a conventional heating-cooling system. In as few as four years, however, proponents claim, the extra cost could be recovered in fuel savings. "ACES is not a cure-all," says Gerald S. Leighton, an ERDA expert on energy use in buildings. "But in some parts of the country it will be another heating and cooling system option in ten years."

In a joint project with Honeywell Inc. and the New York City Housing Authority, ERDA is testing a new control valve for old radiators. The valve would turn on and off automatically to assure a steady, fuel-conserving temperature in old steam-heated buildings with radiators controlled by manual valves. ERDA officials think the new valve could save 15 percent to 20 percent of the heating costs of such buildings. Leighton says the test is an attempt to help market existing technology "by putting the ERDA Good Housekeeping Seal of Approval on it." Of energy saving, he says, "research is the easiest part; commercialization of energy-saving products will be our toughest area."

ERDA is promoting a method of reducing air drag on long-haul trucks to improve fuel economy by as much as 20 percent. In 1976, the agency planned to demonstrate various curved plastic and metal shapes that can be attached to the roof of a truck cab to streamline a rig and keep air from being sucked down between cab and trailer, creating drag. The devices are available; they have not sold because truckers are skeptical of their efficacy.

ERDA is financing a joint effort by Mack Trucks Inc. and Thermo Electron Corporation to improve trucking-fuel efficiency in a more exotic way. The companies are developing a system to recycle back into the engine of a diesel truck the wasted heat that belches out of its exhaust stack at a temperature of 900 degrees.

ERDA also is doing research on advanced automobile engines and on electric cars. In one project, scientists at the Argonne National Laboratory in Illinois are developing a new, more durable battery using lithium and sulfur instead of lead and acid. More powerful batteries would allow electric cars to travel more than 150 miles without a battery recharge. Those cars now being tested by ERDA run down after twenty or thirty miles, and a full recharge requires twelve hours.

22

Sugar from Waste

Leo A. Spano is a jolly sort with a broad grin. One thing he gets a big kick out of is the small jar of glucose crystals on his desk. His associates made the sugar out of some old copies of the *Boston Globe*.

If that seems funny, you should meet Charles R. Wilke of Berkeley, California. Wilke has been turning copies of the *Wall Street Journal* into sugar and the sugar into ethanol, a process that someday may help reduce reliance on petroleum.

Spano and Wilke are chemical engineers. Spano works for the Army at its scientific facilities in Natick, Massachusetts. Wilke is at the University of California. Their efforts, and others', to perfect new methods of making sugar are in earnest, and eventually they may have economic importance. "This is going to be the greatest thing since motherhood," Spano says, running his fingers through the sugar on his desk. "We're taking a renewable resource and making it into a high-energy material that can be used as food or fuel."

That renewable resource is cellulose, the principal material in the cell walls of plants. Cellulose is ubiquitous. It is in trees, crops, and many waste materials, and the sun constantly generates new supplies. Some cellulose is used for energy now, as in wood burning in a stove, and researchers are trying to find ways to make it a more important energy source.

Clayton D. Callihan, a professor of chemical engineering at Louisiana State University, says that some important chemicals and plastics now derived from petroleum—such as polyethylene, polypropylene, styrene, and butadiene—"are going to either disappear or be so expensive that they will find little application in our daily lives." The consequences could be drastic, unless cellulose saves the day. Callihan says, "The obvious replacement for the organic base of these polymers is cellulose because of its perpetual nature."

To derive other useful chemicals from cellulose, one begins with the manufacture of glucose, a form of sugar used in commercial baking. It differs slightly from sucrose, or table sugar. The Army now appears to have the best method of making glucose from cellulose. The method traces its origins to a rotted cotton cartridge belt found in New Guinea during the Second World War. Army scientists found that the belt was being consumed by a greenish-yellow mold, the microorganism *trichoderma viride*. The mold was converting the belt into glucose and consuming it. The Army was interested, of course, because it wanted longer-lasting cartridge belts.

Somebody recalled *t. viride* around 1971, when researchers at Natick started looking for ways to clean up the environment. What better way than to convert waste into something useful? And *t. viride* certainly was able to make useful glucose from cellulosic wastes. Ultimately, the scientists were able, through cobalt radiation, to produce mutations of the microorganism that were more efficient at glucose production than the mold found in nature.

Now the Army is running a full-blown pilot plant with a maze of processing tanks and electrical controls. A young GI spends hour after hour ripping up newspapers to feed into the plant. The conversion process begins when *t. viride* are grown on spruce pulp in a tank of water with nutrients that promote the production of cellulase, an enzyme used to manufacture glucose. The microbes discharge the enzyme into the tank. When the *t. viride* microbes are removed—any left around would gobble up the glucose—what is left is a broth, called "beer," that consists of cellulase and water. Meanwhile, the GI's shredded newsprint has been milled into a grayish powder. Added to the beer, it touches off a chemical process that produces glucose as well as some residues, most of which are filtered out. At this point the glucose is still too impure for human consumption. But it can be used in the manufacture of alcohol and other chemicals. Purified, the glucose was made into a pancake syrup by one researcher.

The Natick project has attracted the interest of scientists around the world. The Soviet Union has bought laboratory equipment to duplicate the effort, and several American corporations, including Gulf Oil Corporation, have begun similar projects on their own.

The Natick results raise the possibility of manufacturing useful chemicals from waste materials as diverse as cow manure, bagasse (the fibrous residue of processed sugar cane), and municipal trash. The wastes from forestry and agriculture alone theoretically could provide 10 percent of the nation's energy, Thomas F. Reed, a chemist formerly at M.I.T., testified at a Senate hearing in 1974.

Projects now under way aim at making ethanol, or ethyl alcohol, from glucose derived from cellulosic waste. The United States consumes more than 300 million gallons of ethanol a year in numerous chemical, toiletry, cosmetic, and other products. The ethanol now comes from ethylene, a petroleum product.

The chemistry of processing ethanol from glucose is well known. Backcountry moonshiners have employed it for hundreds of years. Indeed, before petroleum and ethylene became the major source of ethanol, most of it was produced by yeast fermentation. With the cost of petroleum now running so high, Wilke at the University of California, and Gulf Oil Chemicals Company, independently are attempting to demonstrate that ethanol production by fermentation is again economic on a large scale, mainly because the Natick process is more efficient than earlier methods for producing glucose. "The idea has a lot of moxie to it," says William F. Gauss, a researcher for the Gulf Oil Corporation subsidiary. "If we can pull this off, it will be quite important for the country."

An economic ethanol process could provide the substance as a major ingredient for gasoline, reducing reliance on petroleum for this fuel. Other important chemicals also might be produced from glucose and from ethanol. There are many possibilities in foods. Bechtel Corporation and Louisiana State University have begun a joint venture to make single-cell protein, a possible animal-feed supplement, from bagasse. Scientists at the Natick project say some waste from the conversion process—*t. viride* itself—could be fed to cattle after it has done its job in glucose production. "It's like when you butcher a pig and use everything but the squeal," Spano says.

23

Substituting
Key Materials

Alton McLaughlin is a sprightly, sixty-one-year-old metallurgist for Kaiser Aluminum and Chemical Corporation. He is also something of an alchemist. In a bubbling caldron of pungent hydrochloric acid, he is seeking answers to the problems of turning clays from the earth of Georgia and Alabama into that symbol of consumer affluence, aluminum. Unlike the alchemists of old, who already knew the value of turning lead into gold, McLaughlin is trying to determine if it would be worthwhile to turn clay into aluminum. "The question we must keep asking is, what are the economics?" he says in a laboratory at the Bureau of Mines research center in Boulder City, Nevada.

The search for an economical substitute for bauxite, now the major source of aluminum, has created something of a boom in research at centers such as the small Nevada laboratory, where company metallurgists help and advise government engineers. Together, the aluminum industry and the federal government are supporting this research with some $1.2 million a year.

Stepped-up efforts and expenditures by government and industry aim at developing new sources for other important

146

metals too. Their foreign supply could become tenuous through economic or political developments. Indeed, in 1974, the nations that provide 90 percent of America's bauxite sharply increased their taxes on the ore. Actions by some foreign raw-materials producers in the past few years have smacked of cartelism. Partly as a consequence, there is now "a much higher degree of focus on materials substitution," says Julius Harwood, president of the American Institute of Mining, Metallurgical, and Petroleum Engineers.

Given sufficient incentive, economic or political, there are few materials that cannot be replaced by others. Copper prices can rise high enough to permit the use of expensive palladium and silver in electrical switches. The United States must import all its chromium, used in stainless steel. But manufacturers of products that are chrome-plated for decorative reasons also can use, instead of chrome, a coated plastic that resembles it. And there is a flurry of research into alternatives to stainless steel for many products. Bethlehem Steel is marketing an exhaust pipe material made of carbon, instead of stainless steel; its thin coating of chromium alloy greatly reduces the total amount of chromium in the exhaust-pipe material.

Copper's price escalation in recent years has encouraged intensive research for substitutes. Carrier Corporation, the air-conditioner maker, is using aluminum instead of copper in evaporative coils. The use of plastic piping as a replacement for copper as well as cast iron and steel grew to 1.8 billion pounds in 1974 from only 60 million pounds in 1960. Manmade materials are becoming increasingly useful alternatives to costly imported metals. Plastic and glass fiber are widely used in automobile parts. Chrysler Corporation's spending on research for materials substitutes increased nearly fourfold during the 1970s. PPG Industries Inc. has developed a glass fiber material to compete with steel in such heavy-duty applications as transmission supports.

The greater cost of petroleum products like plastics has lessened their economic attractiveness to some extent since the big leap in the price of oil in the early 1970s. Politics, moreover, often influences the prices of materials. American users of imported materials are vulnerable to politically motivated price manipulation abroad. Higher prices on one material could lead American manufacturers to use a substitute. But a sudden lowering of prices on the material would leave the manufacturers stuck with a supply of the substitute material that is suddenly too costly.

The dilemmas involved in using substitutes are nowhere more evident than in the case of bauxite. Although aluminum is the third most abundant element in the earth's crust, at present it is processed commercially from bauxite alone. The United States has sparse reserves of bauxite. The United States does have nearly inexhaustible reserves of other aluminum-bearing ores, but at present aluminum prices it is uneconomic to process aluminum from them. Thus, American companies must rely on nations with major bauxite deposits, such as Australia, Guinea, and Jamaica. In 1974, major bauxite-producing countries formed a cartel-like organization, the International Bauxite Association, to increase the taxes they collect on bauxite production. Since prices were rising anyway, American consumers of bauxite such as Aluminum Company of America experienced a 100 percent increase in bauxite costs between 1970 and 1974. In 1974 alone, Jamaica led a round of tax increases on bauxite that raised its levy to more than $13 a ton from about $2 a ton.

The bauxite-producing nations, however, have been careful not to price themselves out of the market. The Jamaica increase ultimately jacked up the per-ingot production cost of American aluminum by just 2 cents a pound, leaving a large gap between the relatively low cost of producing aluminum from imported bauxite and the high cost of producing it from native ores. Charles Johnson, an independent minerals economist, figures that Caribbean bauxite can be delivered to the United States for $19 to $27 a ton. To produce the comparable ton of ore in the United States probably would cost more than $40 a ton, he says. Thus Jamaica could double its $13 tax levy before alternate ore technologies could be economically competitive.

Still, says Richard Cole, a Reynolds Metals Company executive, "we're not discouraged." As the price of bauxite goes up, he says, "it's closing the gap." Indeed, the Bureau of

Mines estimates that in 1973, before the most recent foreign tax increases, the cost of running a plant to process alumina (aluminum oxide, smelted into aluminum) from clays was 50 percent higher than comparable bauxite plant costs. By 1976, the cost was estimated at only 20 percent higher.

Clays are only one alternate source of aluminum. There also are esoteric shales and rocks such as anorthosite, alunite, and dawsonite. But all of these sources average only 27 percent alumina content, compared with some 50 percent for bauxite. The lower alumina content requires larger, more complex, and costlier processing equipment that also increases labor and maintenance costs.

Then, too, the processes used for the alternative sources consume at least 50 percent more energy in producing a ton of alumina than the process used for bauxite, according to the Bureau of Mines. It is therefore not surprising that industry is hesitant to invest in a new process, especially in view of its enormous capital investment in existing bauxite plants. As a consequence, not until the 1980s are plants for processing ore other than bauxite expected to be in commercial operation.

Several novel technologies are being researched at the Nevada laboratory. The aim is to select the most likely ore for an experimental government plant that would go on line in the late 1970s. Of the ores being tested in Boulder City and at other research laboratories around the country, clays are rated as the most promising at present. Reynolds Metals, which is building a pilot processing plant in Arkansas, says it holds "hundreds of millions of tons" of clay reserves in the southeastern United States. Some Georgia and Alabama clays contain as much as 38 percent alumina.

Another plant for producing aluminum from clays was scheduled to start up in 1976 in Marseilles, as part of a $30 million, five-year joint research project of Canada's Alcan Aluminum Ltd. and France's Pechiney Ugine Khulman. Anaconda Company is "actively studying" clays, and in 1974 it began trading technology with Alcoa.

Alcoa's major interest, however, lies in anorthosite. The company says that a huge Wyoming deposit of anorthosite rock (containing 27 percent alumina), which it bought in 1972, could hold alumina equal to one-third of the alumina content of the world's known bauxite reserves. A cementlike gel that forms during processing makes the alumina difficult to recover from anorthosite. Alcoa is researching anorthosite processing at a pilot plant in St. Louis, but the company won't discuss its progress publicly.

Alunite was ignored as a source of aluminum until the late 1960s. Deposits of the rock (30 percent alumina) are being tested by Alumet Inc. However, the company is finding it "devilishly hard" to perfect its processing method, says Richard S. Smith, group vice president of National Steel Corporation, a part owner of Alumet. The process, in which the rock is heated, is said to be analogous to "popping popcorn." National Steel is trading alunite technology with the Soviet Union, which already is able to produce alumina from alunite. In 1976, Alumet was considering construction of an alunite refinery in the United States.

Dawsonite is found in large quantities mixed with deep oil shales in Colorado. It holds promise as a source of aluminum. But the shale, which contains about 30 percent alumina, will become an economical source only if it becomes feasible to extract oil from it. As energy costs keep rising, oil-shale production will become more competitive; but then, so will alumina-rich bauxite, shale dawsonite's competitor.

24

Getting About in 2000

Futurists in 1966 had one thing pegged right in their outlook for transportation. Well into the next century, they said, most people still would depend on the automobile and the airplane to move about. But instead of a dazzling, Buck Rogers-like world of plush, electronically controlled ground vehicles and 6,000-mile-an-hour airliners, moving about at the turn of the century will rely on equipment much like that in use now. Today's airline passenger or motorist should be able to step into a vehicle of the early twenty-first century and feel right at home, most experts say. Fundamental changes in design or engineering will be few.

A whole new set of forces has emerged to temper the outlook of the euphoric 1960s. At the time, an unquestioned faith prevailed in the ability of technology to resolve all difficulties. Since then, many people have come to perceive the automobile and the airplane, in their contributions to noise, air, and other pollution, as threats unlikely to be defused merely by turning out fancier cars or faster airplanes.

Environmental worry aside, the availability and cost of petroleum, the sole energy source for cars and airplanes, has deterred fundamental changes in their design. Inflation in costs of research, development, and production has become another and even more forbidding deterrent to radical innova: tion. These factors, along with political and governmental policies, have greatly changed the outlook for transportation over the past ten years.

In 1966, aviation men generally expected that the British-French Concorde supersonic airliner would make its debut in 1971, an American SST in 1975. The SSTs were expected to shrink global travel time in half during the 1970s. Slower jets carrying more than 1,000 passengers each were to succeed the 1970 Boeing 747 jumbo. Such airplanes, which would have been needed to handle a fourfold increase in passenger traffic by 1980, were expected to slash travel costs by the late 1970s to as little as $150 for a round trip by coach between New York and London. It was thought that by the 1990s, 4,000- to 6,000-mile-an-hour hypersonic transports (HSTs) would whisk passengers in suborbital flights between New York and Hong Kong in two hours or less. Fleets of nimble STOLs (short takeoff and landing craft) would bypass airport congestion by using small landing strips in the hearts of big cities.

Today, many airline and aerospace experts consider the SST a fuel-hogging white elephant. The United States killed its SST project five years ago to save money after spending more than $900 million on it. The Concorde made its first commercial flight in 1976, but airlines have ordered only nine of the planes, and the chance is slim that a more feasible second-generation SST will be produced. "We might be wrong," an American aerospace executive says, "but right now we don't have the SST in our models for the airline industry over the rest of the century."

The Boeing 747, with 350 to 400 seats, has proved much too large for many of its intended markets. If larger planes ever come into service, experts say, they will do so ten or fifteen years from now—1986 to 1991—at the earliest. Projections in the mid-1960s were grounded on traffic growth rates then averaging nearly 18 percent a year. Inflation and recession shrank actual growth rates during a more recent five-year period to 3.7 percent a year. "The airlines now are about five years behind the growth that everybody predicted ten years ago," an executive at Lockheed Aircraft Corporation says.

Research on the HST has moved from the back burner to the shelf, though some experts think that in another fifty years or so an HST will be built. The STOL, alive and kicking in the Pentagon, has been almost forgotten by commercial aviation. Economics, air-traffic-control problems, and environmental troubles have all but killed it.

Instead of dropping, air fares are rising steadily, even in noninflated dollars, as productivity gains disappear and cost pressures increase. A round trip New York-London coach ticket cost as much as $806 in the summer of 1976, up 102 percent from $399 just ten years before. Even allowing for the lessened value of the dollar, the increase still amounted to about 30 percent.

Shattered forecasts are common in the automobile industry, too. In 1966, gasoline was cheap, and consumer and industry excitement over cars was at its peak. Although automobile makers knew that critics of cars as sources of congestion, pollution, death, and injury were getting more numerous and vocal, industry experts expected that a well-demonstrated capacity for technical innovation would end all the fears. They were wrong.

If forecasters of a decade ago had been correct, instant communications between cars and central computers, perhaps using satellite transmission, would be directing the flow of traffic on highways to ease congestion. Some cars already might have been equipped with automatic steering and braking and acceleration controls relying on radarlike electronic sensors to avoid crashes. And some cars would have been humming about under pollution-free electric battery power or with clean powerful turbine engines.

A few years from now, small "shopper" cars, their three wheels electrically driven, would be appearing in the suburbs. Big "highway cruisers" would carry families on longer trips. To accommodate all these vehicles, parking areas would be legally required for all new construction. A house, for example, might have to have a five-car garage for the typical five-car family of the year 2000 or thereabouts.

A projection in 1966 called for new-car sales in the United States to rise to at least 22 million units a year by 2000 and perhaps to as many as 25 million, up from 9 million a year at the time. New-car sales rose to a record of 11.4 million in 1973, and they since have fallen.

Some forecasts appear generally to have been on target, though not in quite the same way as envisioned. Car-to-car communication is booming to an extent in the use of citizens'-band radios, especially by truck drivers. General Motors' new Chevette minicar is fairly close, in size at least, to the suburban "shopper."

Other advances simply have failed to come about. The cost of highway construction has become so high that computer-controlled, electronic highways are unfeasible, even though the technology needed to create them has existed for at least ten years. In some other areas, technological advances have been frustratingly slow. For example, research engineers are still trying to build a simple compact system to provide an electric car with just half the speed and range of a mediocre conventional car. Work on turbine cars is continuing, too, but the cost of manufacturing some vital internal parts that would withstand high operating temperatures is still prohibitively high.

Instead of the 25 million cars a year that might have been sold in 2000, forecasters now expect perhaps 17 million or 18 million. Smaller-than-expected population growth, a surge in the cost of car ownership, and the lessened luster of cars as status symbols have shrunk the expected increase in demand. A recent Stanford Research Institute study for Ford Motor Company suggests that "changes in the fundamental lifestyles of Americans" may "affect the way people look upon car ownership and usage." To Lee Iacocca, president of Ford, this means "spending less for things and more for experiences."

Advances in transportation generally are likely to be dictated by technical solutions to problems of fuel consumption, other operating costs, noise, and air pollution. The demand for improved gasoline mileage is probably the weightiest pressure on the automobile industry today, and it may continue so for the rest of the century, regardless of government policy, auto men think. Improving mileage is taking an enormous chunk of the auto industry's financial resources that once were devoted in large part to sales-oriented projects. "Maybe

20 percent of our advanced engineering budget was applied to [exhaust] emissions and fuel economy work ten years ago," a Ford man says. "Now it is about 60 percent."

The same is true of the aircraft industry. "Ten years ago fuel was cheap and plentiful, and there wasn't much interest in obtaining the lowest absolute fuel consumption available," says Bruce N. Torrell, president of Pratt and Whitney, the engine maker. To improve fuel efficiency, engine builders are taking a hard look at several engine designs, even the old turboprop, that were discarded a decade or more ago as obsolete.

Aircraft engine efficiency is rising. Pratt and Whitney says its new JT10D engine, with other aircraft refinements, will increase fuel efficiency by 40 percent or 50 percent and may save 20 percent in direct operating costs in a new generation of 200-seat aircraft to appear by the mid-1980s. Auto manufacturers, too, despite their current protests to the contrary, are likely to achieve by 1985 a federally mandated standard that their cars average 27.5 miles a gallon, twice the 1974 average.

The noise nuisance may speed some innovations in aircraft. "Noise will be the major determining factor in what kinds of new planes are built and when," says Donald Lloyd-Jones, an American Airlines executive. The extent and timing of government action requiring current aircraft to fly more quietly probably will greatly influence equipment buying by airlines in the near future, he says.

Though noise has aroused much of the opposition to SST flights in the United States, experts say technical solutions to the noise problem are at hand. It is the enormous development cost of an SST, and the probable lack of a solution to its fuel-consumption problem, that has dimmed its luster in the view of most American aerospace and airline men.

The experts think the air travel industry will reach its maturity around the 1990s. Before then, they think, there will be one more stage of major technological improvement. This is expected to begin around 1980, when the airlines will replace their then-aging fleets of airplanes such as the Boeing 707 and McDonnell Douglas DC8. The replacements will be smaller than the wide-bodied airplanes of today. In addition to quieter and more efficient engines, their wings will be redesigned, and they will make greater use of high-strength, light-weight materials, new kinds of miniature computers, and other electronic gear to improve control, navigation, and fuel consumption. That, at least, is the expectation. High costs, lack of government aid, and the precarious finances of the airline industry could kill the development of such aircraft. To raise new capital on their own, airlines will have to earn more money than they do now. Otherwise, says Sanford McDonnell, president of McDonnell Douglas Corporation, the capital must come through government nationalization of the industry.

Says Andrew M. De Voursney, top planning executive for United Air Lines: "I question whether our government leaders realize how close this industry may be to nationalization." He estimates that United States airlines will require at least $20 billion in new capital by 1986 to replace their aging fleets and as much as $16 billion by 2000 to handle a modest 5 percent increase in yearly traffic.

High capital costs and pressures for efficiency will work against radical changes in automobiles, too. "The engineering principles on which car designs are based aren't likely to change much between now and 1990," says Craig Marks, a General Motors engineer. Neither, he says, will the basic components of cars change very much. But cars generally will be a lot smaller. By 1980, all types will be at least 20 percent lighter than they are now. Some subtle design changes will improve their aerodynamics. As in aircraft, plastics and other light-weight materials will be more obvious. Yet an amply-sized family sedan will be around, too.

With the possible exception of the electric car, fundamentally new engines won't appear until the 1990s or beyond. Some auto experts think that low-speed, short-range electrical vehicles may be in specialized use before then, however. "Maybe by the year 2000 batteries will be competitive with conventional engines, but I wouldn't bet on it," an engineer says.

By 1986, if De Voursney of United Air Lines is right, only one major commercial aircraft manufacturer will exist in the

United States—Bomac, the survivor of a merger he sees between Boeing and McDonnell Douglas. Lockheed, he and
others believe, will have dropped out of commercial aircraft
manufacture.

By 2000, a few derivatives or successors of the big Boeing
747 may be airborne, carrying 700 to 1,000 passengers. Many
more corporate jets, too, may be flying. Fares will have kept
rising, first-class space on commercial flights will have van-
ished, airplanes will be more crowded, and service will be
more spartan. But airport design, air traffic control, ticketing,
and baggage handling will have improved.

The conventional bus will remain the mainstay of local
transport, though some buses or buslike vehicles may run on
electric power. The grandiose plans for vast, high-speed, ul-
tramodern mass-transit systems are less likely than ever to materialize. "We can build all kinds of mass-transit vehicles," an
expert says, "but no one has yet found what's going to make
people want to get out of their cars and ride them."

Amtrak, the five-year-old government venture that sustains
what's left of the country's intercity rail passenger network,
seems unlikely to survive in its present form. "It's only a matter of time before Congress and the public realize the folly of
pumping billions of tax dollars into a system that serves no
great public purpose and incurs 11 cents in operating costs for
every nickel of revenue it generates," a federal transportation
official says.

Still, Amtrak or a successor may operate high-speed trains
on a few potentially profitable routes like New York-
Philadelphia-Washington, and between such cities "vastly
improved rail mass-transit service at vastly higher speeds" may
be available, according to this official.

At first blush, it seemed that the prospect of increasingly
scarce petroleum supplies and increasingly higher fuel costs
would enhance the future of mass transit. But serious studies
dispute that conclusion. Simply put, the great obstacle to mass
transit is the need to tie up enormous capital twenty-four hours
a day to handle peak loads of only two or three hours. Suburban sprawl and the southwestward drift of population that demographers foresee—it clearly has taken shape in the past ten

years—are other factors in mass transit's fading future. "There's no future for rail mass transit because of the basic requirement of a fixed right of way," says a market planner for an aerospace company that has dabbled in rail transportation for years. "You can't just pick up your track and move it when demand for your service shifts from one route to another."

A number of other major corporations, some with federal money, have plunged into the research and development of mass transit systems and equipment, sometimes called "people movers." Ford Motor Company, for example, designed a system that could serve several stops in a relatively short distance, using a few small coaches on a guideway— something akin to a combination of a subway line and a monorail. Ford has dropped the project because of lack of interest in the transit industry. "I guess you could say our people mover is totally on the shelf," Ford chairman Henry Ford II concludes.

25

The Southwestward Shift

Only a dozen years ago, New York Mayor Robert F. Wagner told his fellow citizens: "The economy of New York City is fundamentally strong and sound. It can only be described in superlatives." In 1976, Roger Starr, then the city's housing and development administrator, took things differently. He said he was sometimes tempted to leave. "If I were young," he pronounced, "I sometimes think I would." Starr is no more sanguine about other cities in the nation's Northeast. And other official and nonofficial experts share his pessimism. In 1966, most of them believed that most cities would continue to boom through the year 2000. The big problem was how to develop space-age technology to manage the growth. Now, the question for many cities is whether they will remain economically and socially viable at all.

As those who are paid to study such things see it, here is the outlook for cities and suburbs through the year 2000:

—Southern and Western cities will enjoy their boom another fifteen years or more, but growth rates thereafter will slump.

—Older Northeastern and Midwestern cities will experience anything from slow growth to disastrous decline. Any decline will blight near-in suburbs, too. But any growth, or even benign stagnation, will strikingly upgrade some central-city residential areas. Even parts of New York's Harlem may become prospering neighborhoods of luxury housing.

—Urban crime will decline, though the drop may not be noticeable for another ten years or so. Murder will not move to the suburbs, but burglary will continue to do so.

—In many cities, ethnic minorities will continue to become majorities. The Bronx borough of New York City may become more than 90 percent black and Puerto Rican. Though whites' fear of minorities will die slowly, minorities themselves will become increasingly bourgeois.

—Nearly everywhere, outlying suburbs will thrive.

—Dispersal of population will remain the major urban trend through the year 2000.

If the urban economic outlook is more somber than ten years ago, birth control is a big part of the reason. Then, most seers thought the United States population would soar to about 340 million by 2000. Nearly all cities would keep growing, it was expected, even though some would grow a great deal more than others. Now, however, lower birthrates have sharply reduced population estimates to between 245 million and 287 million at the turn of the century, up from 214 million today. This means that Houston's growth may come at Cleveland's expense.

Even as many cities lose population, the nation will become more urban. The Regional Plan Association, a New York research group, predicts that 40 percent of all Americans in 2020 will live in metropolitan areas of more than 2.5 million people, up from 21 percent today. Growth will come mainly in suburbs and in cities of the Southern and Western sun belt.

Economics will continue to encourage industry to move out of cities. Leonard C. Yaseen, chairman of Fantus Company, a major plant-location consulting firm, has calculated the costs of staying in the city versus moving. By locating outside a big city, he says, a company typically can cut its geographically variable costs, such as labor, taxes, and utilities, by 25 percent to 35 percent for factories, 12 percent to 20 percent for clerical operations, and 5 percent to 8 percent for corporate headquarters.

The advantages that promoted locating in the cities in the first place are disappearing, many experts say. Some companies chose city locations for their rail connections and access to water transport. Today, the same concerns rely mainly on trucking. Communications improvements have lessened the value of the face-to-face dealing that helped draw commerce to cities. And automobile ownership has diminished the importance of locations near mass-transit terminals.

Most city locations do not permit the straight long one-story assembly lines that modern plants use, Yaseen says. "And even elevator makers don't want to use multistory plants any more," he observes. He thinks that by 2000, New York City will have lost about half its current number of jobs. While many businesses in older cities like New York will have moved to outlying suburbs, other concerns will have gone South or West. These regions got 82 percent of new manufacturing jobs in the past five years, he says.

Some cities that Yaseen and others expect to grow especially fast over the next twenty-five years are Denver; Dallas; Houston; Phoenix; Salt Lake City; Portland, Oregon; Jackson, Mississippi; Tampa; St. Petersburg; Santa Ana, California; and Greenville, South Carolina. Yet in another fifteen years, the growth of these cities, too, may slow considerably. John W. Dyckman, professor of planning at the University of Southern California in Los Angeles, thinks supply and demand will tend to equalize labor and other costs throughout the country. As it is now, the South and the West generally experience fewer strikes, pay lower wages, and enjoy lower living costs, as well as warmer weather, than the Northeast.

Because their economies are soundly diversified, Chicago and Philadelphia will remain stable and slow-growing. Or so believes Peter D. Salins, chairman of the urban affairs department at New York's Hunter College. The New York area, too, will grow slowly, and it will remain the nation's financial and cultural center, he says; the city's fiscal ailments are not necessarily chronic. San Francisco and Boston, Salins says, will "trade on their charm" and remain "our answers to Copenhagen." Denver, Seattle, Minneapolis-St. Paul, and Portland, Oregon, will keep their reputations as "healthy, good places to live."

Sick cities of the future, among others, are Detroit, St. Louis, and Cleveland, Salins says. Problem cities will be those that have relied on a few heavy industries that are decentralizing or retrenching, he adds. Such cities have exceptionally severe social problems; last year, for example, Detroit and Cleveland had twice the homicide rate of New York and Los Angeles.

Other experts offer similar, though not identical, city-by-city forecasts. Within metropolitan areas, too, the experts expect significant changes. The New York metropolitan area now is the home of 16 million people. Salins says the population will rise to about 18 million by the year 2000, but it will stagnate at just under 8 million in New York City itself, and Manhattan, the commercial and financial center of the city, will lose some 400,000 of its current 1.5 million residents.

Yet in doing so, Manhattan may prosper. Salins thinks the population decline mainly will reflect smaller households. The kind of people who often choose to live in places like Manhattan are increasing in numbers: single people who have left their parents, small young families, families with two incomes, couples postponing children, and divorced people. "Every divorce," Salins observes, "creates a need for two apartments."

In the journal *New York Affairs,* Salins recently wrote that Manhattan will "become chic-er and less populous as the rich, the single, the eccentric and the hip . . . drive out the ethnic, the poor and the fertile."* Already under way, an expansion in the luxury rental market in Manhattan may turn nearly all of residential Manhattan south of Harlem, and parts of Harlem itself, into high-rent districts. Similar trends, Salins thinks, will occur in other metropolitan areas of more than 500,000 people.

* "New York in the Year 2000," *New York Affairs,* Vol. 1, No. 4 (Spring 1974), p. 6.

The poor will disperse in a pattern that may seem erratic. Salins expects many to keep moving to the Bronx, whose population now is classed as 27 percent poor. The proportion of poor by the turn of the century, he says, will reach 40 percent in the Bronx, and "the south Bronx [just across the Harlem River from Harlem] will be a real sea of pathology and misery for a long, long time." Brooklyn, he thinks, also will become well over half black and Puerto Rican. But he predicts that the borough will be markedly more stable than the Bronx, partly because it has more private homes and is more likely to attract middle-class minority members. Other New York City boroughs will retain white majorities, Salins believes.

Though blacks and Puerto Ricans will continue to move to built-up near-in suburbs, they will remain less likely than whites to become suburbanites. Instead, most authorities think, minorities increasingly will form a new urban middle class. But sluggish economic growth may hinder this upward mobility, and most experts believe that the central cities of the year 2000 still will have a large underclass of jobless residents who pay little in taxes but use many public services.

"This problem is likely to endure in its more severe forms for as long as fifty years and maybe even longer," says Henry Cohen, dean of the Center for New York City Affairs at the New School for Social Research in New York. Edward C. Banfield, Harvard professor of government, thinks that the current social problems of big cities will persist in their present form for at least another twenty years.

Barring a fundamental change in the demographic characteristics of criminals, many experts foresee a leveling-off or a decrease in violent crime. By 1990, says Marvin E. Wolfgang, a University of Pennsylvania criminologist, the age group from fourteen to twenty-four will make up only about 15 percent of the population, against about 21 percent today. This, he says, is "of overwhelming importance" because young males account for most violent crime. James Q. Wilson, Harvard professor of government and an expert on crime, expects city crime rates to keep rising for a few years more and then to fall as the population ages. He thinks burglary may rise in the suburbs, but violence there will remain far less common than in the city.

"A crime of stealth can be perpetrated wherever the mode of transportation permits it, and the suburban home is ideally designed from the burglar's point of view. But crimes of violence tend to occur where there is a subculture of violence." In their physical appearance, cities are expected to change far less by 2000 than was predicted in the *Wall Street Journal* and elsewhere ten years ago. Hope for a breakthrough that would produce new, superfast, economically feasible mass transit systems generally is fading. The dispersal of jobs and housing will make the family automobile, as small as it may become, more important than it is even now. Interest in "new towns," communities planned and engineered as urban utopias, was widespread ten years ago. Today, as population forecasts sag, talk of new towns also is diminishing. And because of population and job dispersal, the era of 100-story buildings also may have died.

Some factors will work to slow, though not halt, the process of dispersal. High energy costs may give public transportation, and cities, a fresh economic appeal. And once all the companies that can benefit from doing so have moved out of cities, the business that remains is likely to be healthily entrenched. Public policy, too, just might alter the general downward course of the bigger older cities, though many authorities doubt its effectiveness. Toronto, Cincinnati, Minneapolis, Kalamazoo, Michigan, and others have bolstered their downtowns through sophisticated zoning and planning.

A rise in individual purchasing power may offset part of the economic impact of central-city population losses. And finally, some experts hope, an unforeseen development could produce a striking renaissance in the older cities. Alluding to Vermont's ski boom, the former New York City official Roger Starr said, "I just keep hoping somebody will invent the urban equivalent of the ski."

26

Leaving New York

Faced with such immediate problems as how to meet the next payroll, New York's Mayor Abraham Beame has little time to worry about the long term. But even if the city surmounts its current financial crisis, its economic future may grow grimmer by the day. Students of the city's economy see its future chiefly as a center for large corporate offices, the communications industry, and the finance business. Manufacturing employment in the city has been dwindling since the Second World War. Yet in the past decade thousands of nonmanufacturing jobs have disappeared as scores of companies have moved their headquarters or major operations out of the city. And the exodus shows no sign of abating soon.

"I wouldn't worry about the outflow by itself; there's a similar trend toward decentralization in all major metropolitan areas," says Dick Netzer, dean of the Graduate School of Public Administration at New York University. "What worries me is that there is so little inflow."

The exodus deprives the city of both corporate and individual taxpayers, at the same time that the decrease in job opportunities is adding to welfare costs. The departures include companies of all sizes, but it is the largest that have attracted the most attention.

"In 1966, of *Fortune* magazine's 1,000 largest American industrial companies, 198 were headquartered in Manhattan," says Leonard C. Yaseen, chairman of Fantus Company, plant-location consultants. "In the ten years since then, the list has dropped to 120. A few have gone out of business, some have merged, but fifty-five of these major corporations actually left the city."

The future isn't entirely bleak. New York still has far more major corporate headquarters than any other city; it even has added a few, such as Norton Simon Inc. and General Instrument Corporation. The securities industry, after shrinking sharply in recent years, may be stabilizing along with the national economy and the stock market. Six of the nation's ten largest commercial banks are in New York City, and the banks added a total of 10,000 jobs between 1969 and 1974.

On balance, the job picture is mixed. Herbert Bienstock, who heads the Bureau of Labor Statistics office in New York, recently reported that the city lost a total of 340,000 jobs in the 1969–1974 period, almost wiping out the gain of 349,000 jobs of the previous fifteen years. The decline, he said, reflected a sharp acceleration in the rate of factory job losses as well as substantial job losses in nonmanufacturing industries, the source of the net job growth in New York City during the 1960s.

"In 1950," Yaseen says, "industrial jobs in the five boroughs of New York represented almost 7 percent of the nation's manufacturing work force. Today, this percentage has dropped to barely 3 percent, and within ten years, New York City's share of factory employment may well fall below 1 percent of the U.S. total."

The decline of manufacturing in part reflects changing technology. Most of New York's factories are multistory buildings, and manufacturers have found they can operate more efficiently in single-story plants stretching over large acreage, the sort of acreage that is scarce in the city except at high prices and high tax rates. Diminished national rail service has encouraged companies to switch to trucks, which are hard to move through the city's narrow and congested streets.

Of course, New York is not the only city that is losing manufacturing jobs. Most economists regard the movement of factories out of antiquated facilities in the cities as a natural evolutionary process. Less than 1 percent of Manhattan's factory space has been built since 1945. But the trend has occurred in a period when New York City's work force has become increasingly composed of Puerto Ricans, blacks, and other minority-group members, many of them ill-equipped for the office jobs that planners hoped would take up the employment slack.

"The people we have need a generation or two to develop the skills needed for jobs in corporate offices, finance, and the communications industries," a business-association official says. "Within fifteen years we may have a sufficiently large pool of such people." Like a lot of other people worried about New York's present and future, this official prefers not to be quoted by name. The city's troubles are so deeply involved in politics that many businessmen would rather not express their views publicly. "When it comes to New York City, we try to keep a low profile," says an economist for a major New York bank.

But some of the businesses that have moved out in recent years, or soon will, are willing to disclose their reasoning. Nearly all of them emphasize that the city retains large advantages as a center of transportation, finance, communications, and cultural activities. They stress that their departure decisions have had little to do with New York's fiscal turmoil. And in nearly all cases, the companies have retained sizable offices in New York City.

Not surprisingly, most of the former New Yorkers have chosen locations close to the city in New Jersey, Westchester County, or Connecticut. John Mitovich, president of the Stamford Area Commerce and Industry Association in Connecticut, says that the Stamford-Greenwich area now has the headquarters of 17 of *Fortune* magazine's 500 largest industrial companies, "ranking it third behind New York and Chicago."

What prompts corporations to move out of New York? In talks with officials of a score of major corporations, the factor most often cited is the difficulty of inducing their middle-level management employees to move from elsewhere in the

United States to jobs in a New York City headquarters, even though the moves involve promotions and pay increases.

"Some of the younger management people we were bringing in found they couldn't get acceptable housing, either in the city or within what they thought was a reasonable commuting distance," says George W. Griffin, Jr., vice president of public affairs of General Telephone and Electronics Corporation. "The percentage of acceptances of promotions to headquarters went down. After we announced our move, the acceptances went back up again." In June 1973, GTE moved into a new $30 million building in an urban redevelopment area in downtown Stamford.

GTE's giant competitor, American Telephone and Telegraph Company, plans to keep its corporate headquarters in downtown New York. By the end of 1975, however, AT&T had made plans to move 3,400 employees into new facilities in Basking Ridge, New Jersey, and the key reason was the same as GTE's. "We draw personnel from units of the Bell System around the country—rotational personnel, who come in to headquarters for a time," said Robert D. Lilly, then head of AT&T. "A generation ago these middle-management personnel stood in line to come to New York. In recent years, many have refused to come. They liked suburban living. Many had small children, and they didn't like the cost of private schools in New York."

Holding on to middle management is one of many reasons for leaving the city. An executive of a company now considering a move rather easily made up a list of fifteen reasons. Actually, two of his reasons—greater personal safety and better security—pretty much overlap and, in one form or another, show up on the lists of all departees.

General Electric Company was "highly visible and vulnerable to demonstrations and violence" in New York City, says Frank Donovan, a GE official involved in moving the company's headquarters to Fairfield, Connecticut, in August 1974. The New York building was emptied several times by bomb threats. Three bombs were found in the building, and one exploded.

New York City itself, of course, is always highly visible in the nation's news media. Bombings and street violence in

New York are likely to get more national attention than similar events in a Midwestern city and thus may play a role in the worries of those middle managers. Another factor, though, is that many companies in New York City had grown so rapidly since World War II that their employees were scattered among several buildings, complicating security problems. "We were in several buildings in New York," says John E. Kircher, the head of Continental Oil Company. "We had to consolidate either in the city or outside. We made the decision in the 1970–1971 period, when rents were very high in New York." Conoco moved in February 1972 to a new building in High Ridge Park, a collection of corporate offices in Stamford.

Although rents have since come down in New York, suburban-versus-city costs were a consideration with all of the corporate expatriates. General Telephone says that it could not have duplicated a new building in New York for anything like its Stamford cost. Several companies that had rented space in New York City contended that they were, in effect, paying double property taxes. The rents they paid landlords were used to pay property taxes. And then the city imposed on tenants a "commercial occupancy tax" that ranges up to 7.5 percent of rental payments.

The former New Yorkers still must deal with labor unions. Thus none of them want to be quoted in opposition to the New York State law that permits unemployment compensation to be paid to strikers after a waiting period. But several noted that Rhode Island is the only other state where such a law exists.

New York commuting frustrations figured in the thinking of all the expatriates. "In New York we couldn't start a meeting until 9:30," Conoco's Kircher says, "and at 5 P.M. everyone was looking at his watch." At GE, employees now work from 8:15 A.M. to 5 P.M., and executives are sure that productivity has risen because of the absence of commuting problems.

None of the companies that has left or is considering leaving believes that the step will resolve every problem. At most suburban offices all or nearly all employees drive to work. Although total commuting time in most cases is much less, the traffic problems in several areas are growing. AT&T is giving driving lessons to New York employees who will operate cars for the first time in getting to the Basking Ridge facility.

All the expatriates say they have been highly successful in holding on to employees through their moves, not only executives but also most clerical workers, and none admits to any problems in hiring new help locally. For several months after Olin Corporation moved from New York to Stamford, the company operated three buses from New York. "We still have some people commuting here from the city," says T. J. Olsen, vice president. But the company's outside directors have not been so easily converted to Connecticut. "We still hold all board meetings in New York," Olsen says. So do some other companies.

The former New Yorkers are all aware that New York City and New York State personal taxes are the country's highest, and thus they were a burden on employees. But no one identifies this as a major factor in moving. "After all," an executive says, "New Jersey and Connecticut are having their own budget problems now."

In many areas, shortages of restaurants and first-class hotels are an annoyance. After bragging about the efforts his company had made to install fine dining facilities in its building, one executive took a visitor to lunch in the place the executive preferred—a restaurant five miles away.

Companies that have left the city bend over backward to become good citizens of their new communities. Olin, for instance, dug up, stored, and replanted several large trees that were in the way of construction at its site in Stamford. General Electric sits atop a hill near the Merritt Parkway in Fairfield, and a company official says that GE has beautified the site. "Before we came," he says, "the topsoil had been ripped off this hill, and it was used as an obstacle course for motorcycles." GE also donated part of the land it purchased to the town of Fairfield as parkland.

Kircher of Conoco thinks that rising costs of energy conceivably could stop the move to the suburbs or even reverse it. Scattering offices across the countryside and putting nearly all employees in their own cars obviously are not the most efficient ways to use energy. For the present, however, if the decision were to be made again, Kircher and the other former New Yorkers say that it would be the same.

27

The Automated Battlefield

Not long after the latest Mideast war, Malcolm Currie, the Pentagon's research and development chief, sketched for Congress his vision of war in the future. Tactical advances, he said, foreshadowed "a true revolution in conventional warfare." Some of the new technology, in its Model-T stages, already has been proved in combat: unerring, precision-guided bombs and missiles, unmanned aircraft, remote electronic sensors. "Advances such as these, further developed and widely applied," he said, "can change a broad spectrum of conventional warfare in the next decade, in the way tanks once revolutionized ground combat and radar revolutionized air defense."

Yet only ten years ago, in 1966, military experts failed to foresee the automated battlefield that already is becoming a reality. The technology was understood, but the war in Vietnam accelerated actual development much faster than anyone would have guessed. Nor was that all the experts missed. They failed to anticipate most diplomatic, political, and economic developments that have had a profound influence on military thinking and planning. They had no notion of an agreement between the Soviet Union and the United States to limit offensive nuclear weapons, or of detente generally. They had little hint that American involvement in Vietnam would create a strong antimilitary mood, ending for at least half a decade near-automatic congressional approval of defense budgets. Nor was there any sign that the United States would abandon the draft in favor of costly volunteer forces and that manpower expenses would consume 55 percent of the defense budget.

Finally, the experts were unable to foresee the explosion in the cost of modern weaponry fostered by inflation, the increasing complexity of weaponry, and production problems. In 1967, weapons planners usually assumed that if something new and exotic could be built, it would be built. Today, cost constraints threaten to keep many futuristic plans on the drawing boards. Thus Pentagon experts are more cautious in their long-range predictions than their predecessors in the mid-1960s.

The United States is unlikely to become a garrison state. By 2000, a Pentagon forecast has it, military budgets probably will use up less of the gross national product than they do today—less than 5 percent compared with the current 6 percent. Inflation will eat up much of the dollar increase, so that many analysts believe that American forces will number fewer than today's 2.1 million uniformed men and women. In any case, a simple projection of current cost trends is unthinkable. If they do continue for a few more decades, says Army undersecretary Norman Augustine, "we will quite literally be able to afford only one aircraft or, for that matter, one tank and one ship." "Cost is a huge consideration," says an Army general who oversees research and development. "We just have to consider the affordability of these modern technologies."

Still, much of the military hardware that will be in use at the turn of the century is already visible in research and development centers, because it can take fifteen years to move a complex new creation from the research stage to active duty. Twenty-five years hence, defense experts expect, strategic nuclear weapons, designed to deter atomic war, still will enjoy top priority. The arsenal is likely to consist, as it does today, of a mixture of land-based missiles, submarine-launched missiles, and long-range bombers. But there will be important new departures.

Today's Minuteman III intercontinental ballistic missile will be supplemented by the larger M-X, a missile that may be more mobile and so less vulnerable. The giant Trident submarine, just going into production, will be the backbone of the undersea strategic force. The B1 bomber, if moved into production as scheduled, will still be on duty, although it could be beefed up with highly accurate cruise missiles—jet-powered computer-guided missiles that fly low and slow to escape radar detection.

For conventional ground warfare, the Army will have a new tank and a new mechanized combat vehicle that, in effect, allows an infantry squad to fight while riding. It will have electrically guided artillery shells that can easily hit moving tanks, a heat-sensitive infrared sensor system that allows soldiers to "see" through darkness and smoke, and "instant minefields" that can be fired by artillery or aircraft on advancing enemy troops.

The Air Force still will man fighter planes. But unmanned aircraft, called remotely piloted vehicles (RPVs), will fly many reconnaissance and bombing missions, and some might be ready for air-to-air combat. Weapons delivered by the planes and RPVs will be much smarter than today's "smart" bombs, able to find and destroy their targets at night and in bad weather. Earth-orbiting satellites probably will help guide them.

Naval warfare seems less likely to change. At any rate, many American admirals insist that large nuclear-powered aircraft carriers should continue to be built at a cost of nearly $2 billion each. Still, experts in and out of government think that the day of the giant carrier is nearing an end, and the search for a replacement is on. A Navy study suggests that the substitute will be a relatively austere "air-capable" ship of about 10,000 tons that would be armed with antiship and antiaircraft missiles and vertical-takeoff fighter planes.

Even as they plan these and other weapons, however, defense officials have nagging doubts that they are preparing for the right kind of war. Ever since the withdrawal from Vietnam, the military establishment has turned its attention toward a possible land war in Central Europe, where thirty years after the Second World War, 600,000 European soldiers and 200,000 American GIs still face 915,000 Soviet-led troops. "For the foreseeable future we will continue to shape our forces against the only guys who pose a substantial threat," an assistant defense secretary says. "But the sophisticated weapons we're developing to take on the Soviets aren't the ones I would want for trouble with India or Panama."

Indeed, many defense analysts believe that the greatest danger to the United States in the closing years of the century will come from poorer, less industrial nations, and most likely in the form of terrorism rather than conventional warfare. "Between now and the year 2000, I think there is a major opportunity for a shift from East-West confrontation to North-South confrontation," an Air Force strategist says. "We've already seen the first evidence of this—in plane hijackings, kidnappings, and mail bombs."

In his study, *Transnational Terror,* J. Bowyer Bell, a researcher at Columbia University's Institute of War and Peace Studies, found the United States a likely target of foreign terrorism. "Revolutionaries from abroad, attracted by soft targets, may strike at what they see as the center of the imperialist-capitalist-racist conspiracy," he said.*

Large, complex industrial societies are increasingly vulnerable to the new generation of small, easy-to-operate, highly accurate missiles. Brian Jenkins, an analyst at the RAND Corporation think tank, says such weapons "will undoubtedly find their way into the hands of terrorists." He asks: "What will happen when the 'Saturday night special' is not a revolver but perhaps a hand-held laser-guided missile?"

A special horror is the prospect of terrorists armed with nuclear weapons, raising the specter of what Jenkins calls "political extortion and mass-hostage situations on a scale that we have not yet seen." Other researchers worry about outright nuclear warfare touched off by the proliferation of nuclear

* Policy Study 17, The American Enterprise Institute for Public Policy Research, Washington, D.C., and the Hoover Institution on War, Revolution and Peace, Stanford University, Stanford, California (September 1975), p. 87.

weapons. Five members of a Harvard University-Massachusetts Institute of Technology study group concluded last year that nuclear war is likely to erupt before 1999, most probably between smaller nations in the Mideast or Africa.

"There are going to be an awful lot of people with nuclear weapons, and it's going to be awfully important to be able to intercept one or two of those weapons," a top Army official says. By a 1972 treaty, the United States and the Soviet Union each limited itself to a single antiballistic missile (ABM) site, and the United States now is abandoning its site in North Dakota. Some analysts believe that the United States eventually will have to build new ABM defenses against threats from terrorists and smaller powers.

An Air Force general thinks an answer to such threats may lie in high-energy laser weapons, based in space, capable of destroying missiles with thin, powerful light beams. The Pentagon is spending some $200 million a year to develop more powerful lasers. In this and in other research and development, however, defense officials are encountering serious technical and cost problems.

Such problems befell certain weapons projects described in the 1967 look by the *Wall Street Journal* at war in the future. At the time, the MBT-70 "dream" tank, for example, was to go into service in the early 1970s. After nine years of development, Congress killed it in December 1971. The House Appropriations Committee saw it as "unnecessarily complex, excessively sophisticated, and too expensive." It would have cost $1 million a vehicle, and, the committee said, "no tank is worth that much money."

Most experts assume that the United States and the Soviet Union will not fight a nuclear war. But the strategic arms race, they think, will continue, only slightly slowed by arms control agreements. The United States is modernizing its entire arsenal of long-range weapons. It is spending $2.5 billion to research and develop an intercontinental ballistic missile more powerful and less vulnerable than the Minuteman III.

Decisions on how and where to base the new M-X missiles will be tricky. Three alternatives are under consideration: hardened underground silos like those housing the Minuteman, mobile "transporters-launchers," and large aircraft. The Air Force explored the latter alternative by dropping a Minuteman I from a C5A cargo plane and igniting the missile in midair. Completion in 1984 of a new system of twenty-four NAVSTAR communications-navigation satellites would improve the accuracy of that kind of delivery system.

The shape of the next generation of missile-firing submarines and long-range bombers is clearer. General Dynamics already has contracts for construction of the first three of ten Trident submarines. The huge nuclear-powered Tridents, to be launched by the end of the 1970s, each will carry twenty-four nuclear missiles with ranges of 4,000 miles at first and 6,000 miles in later versions. The current cost of each submarine with missiles is more than $1.5 billion.

The new bomber will be Rockwell International's B1, barring abandonment of the controversial aircraft by some future Congress or president. Critics think that the B1 is obsolete already and that, at nearly $87 million per plane, it costs too much anyway. But the first test bomber flew in late 1974, and the Air Force is pushing for a production go-ahead late in 1976.

On the ground, the 1973 Arab-Israeli war most convincingly illustrated the potential of the kind of automated combat born in Vietnam. Many Western military observers saw in the Mideast war the emerging superiority of new defensive weapons against the tanks and fighter-bombers that had dominated battlefields since the Second World War.

One of the Army's most striking advances is a laser-guided artillery shell known as the cannon-launched guided projectile. It promises to make tanks even more vulnerable in the future than they are now. They would be targeted by small unmanned aircraft with television cameras and laser beams. The projectile would home in on the laser-designated target. In tests, the shell has hit a moving M48 tank. In effect, it would turn artillery into sniper weaponry.

The world got its first sustained look at similarly guided airborne projectiles in Vietnam. A designator aircraft would focus a laser beam on a target, and a second plane would drop a "smart" bomb, equipped with a device to sense laser light reflected from the target and adjust the bomb's steering vanes toward it. Such precision-guided weapons today can hit targets 50 miles to 100 miles distant, but not in fog or darkness. In the future, they will operate in any kind of weather. And they may be programmed to choose targets: a tank, say, rather than a mere jeep.

At sea, Navy men think that twenty-five years hence, one of their prime missions will be the protection of surface shipping for a nation that will be importing even more raw materials, especially oil, and exporting even more agricultural and industrial products.

The high cost of building superfast warships, and technical and other difficulties, have dimmed their lustre. Some Navy men suspect that the basic warship of the future may resemble a rather unspectacular design, the ACV-G, or advanced aviation-guided missile combatant. Essentially it would be a box 450 feet long, 150 feet wide, and four stories high, riding out of the water on two submarinelike structures. Its open decks could launch a dozen vertical-takeoff planes, and it would be armed with antiship, antiaircraft, and antisubmarine missiles. Its top speed would be forty knots.

Summary

Remember the rolamite?

In all history, by one count, only 27 elementary mechanisms, such as the lever, the pulley, the ball joint, the hinge, and the clutch, have been invented. The twenty-seventh was the rolamite, the only one to appear in this century. It came on the scene only in 1967. In its basic form, the rolamite consists of two metal cylinders, each snugged into one crook of an S-shaped flexible metal band under tension. Because the cylinders will move almost instantaneously in response to minute changes in pressure or temperature on the S-band, the cheap and practically indestructible rolamite could replace the working parts of hundreds of more complicated and costly mechanical devices.

It has not, however, done so. Manufacturers admire the rolamite's elegance but are unwilling to invest the capital or revamp their operations to make things with it. And while the rolamite could make, among hundreds of other things, a better mousetrap, nobody is beating a path to the inventor's door.

Perhaps someday they will. Meanwhile, there is a lesson in the rolamite. Technological advance alone may be insufficient to resolve the huge and baffling problems in resource management that are confronting American industry.

Of all these problems, the energy "crisis," even if temporarily abated, appears the most enormous. Neither America nor the rest of the world is expected to run out of energy, as some pessimistic projections have suggested. But there is practically no hope that the once-envisioned age of cheap, abundant nuclear energy will ever dawn.

As a consequence, the economic management of existing energy resources and the development of new sources has become critical. Solar power, already economic in some small-scale applications, may provide an increasing share of the nation's power, perhaps as much as 15 percent by the year 2000. Only if plutonium breeder reactors are proved economical will nuclear power provide as much as 28 percent of the nation's energy by 2000, and there are serious doubts that such reactors are feasible. The world's oil probably will begin running out by the end of this century.

One expert whose views are reported in the foregoing section suggests that by 2000, "the biggest revolution in energy will be in the business of energy consumption." If energy costs continue to rise as expected, the market for products and processes that consume little energy in their use or manufacture will expand. Here and there throughout the country, technical-minded people are heating and cooling their homes with solar power, buying bicycles, and dispensing with some electrical appliances. Perhaps an entire generation of Americans, faced with spiraling utility bills, will learn to ration their electricity and natural gas. In New York, Consolidated Edison is already promoting an experiment in which homeowners and apartment dwellers can take part. The customers who cooperate are maximizing their energy usage in off-peak-load hours and minimizing it in peak-load hours to determine just how much they can reduce energy demand and costs.

That kind of rational energy consumption is independent of high technology. In transportation, too, expensive technology appears to provide no solution to the energy problem because "inflation in costs of research, development, and production has become another and . . . forbidding deterrent to radical innovation." Airplanes and automobiles use petroleum as their sole energy source. As it becomes increasingly scarce and costly, research and development is being aimed at efficiency rather than the creation of a "dazzling, Buck Rogers-like world of plush, electronically controlled ground vehicles and 6,000-mile-an-hour airliners." With its inflexible right of way and huge capital cost, rapid transit is quickly losing its allure as the people mover of the future.

Whatever its costs in manufacture and energy consumption, the automobile will continue as America's favorite form of transportation. Indeed, in that area where the automobile is a necessity rather than a luxury—the "sun belt" of the South and West—the American population is increasing fastest. As several of the preceding chapters suggest, the economic growth of the South and West, along with certain parts of the Midwest, will outstrip the rest of the nation for quite a while.

As people migrate to the thriving sun belt and create new consumer markets and pools of labor, so will large corporations. Between 1966 and 1975, fifty-five corporations on *Fortune* magazine's list of the thousand largest moved their headquarters from New York City. Although most of them have moved to nearby suburban locations, a few left for the Southeast and elsewhere, and more will do so in the next few decades.

Whatever the specific reasons that corporations give for relocating, they are all essentially related to a search for improved communications and greater efficiency in the use of energy, land, labor, and transportation. True, efficiency never has been far from the minds of most competent corporate managers, but during the infatuation of the 1960s with technical innovation and creative finance, it sometimes seemed less important than selling "concepts" to securities analysts. Efficiency was taken for granted.

No more. The old-line engineer may come into his own again in the management of American corporations as the importance of efficiency in resource utilization grows. Even in the distasteful business of war, as the concluding chapter of this book shows, efficiency has become the single most important goal of defense managers. The capital costs of improved weaponry, including their research and development, have become so huge that defense planners are seriously concerned that "we will quite literally be able to afford only one aircraft or, for that matter, one tank and one ship."

In a world once perceived as overladen with natural riches, such thinking may seem medieval. Still, the careless and wasteful use of resources that characterized the past will end. As long as American business remains competitive, corporations that cannot oblige the demand for efficiency will not survive.

Sources

The following list gives the authors and titles of all the *Wall Street Journal* articles on which this book is based.

JERRY E. BISHOP, "Gaining on Death: Drugs Are Emerging as Powerful Weapons for Fighting Cancer," April 1, 1976.

MARY BRALOVE, "Working Partners: For Married Couples, Two Careers Can Be Exercise in Frustration," May 13, 1975.

DAVID BRAND, "The Food Crisis: New-Food Research Isn't Likely to Ease Poor Nations' Hunger," December 18, 1974.

DAVID BRAND, "Power Pioneers: Some Small Innovators Heat Homes by Sun, Light Them by Wind," March 18, 1975.

LINDLEY H. CLARK, JR., "The Exodus: New York, Which Sees Office Jobs as Key to Future, Loses Them," June 5, 1975.

TODD FANDELL and CHARLES CAMP, "The Future Revised: Transportation in 2000 to Rely on Equipment Much Like Today's," April 1, 1976.

LIZ ROMAN GALLESE, "The Soothsayers: More Companies Use 'Futurists' to Discern What Is Lying Ahead," March 31, 1975.

LES GAPAY, "Better Ideas: Energy Research Agency Is Promoting Ways, Like New Kind of Light Bulb, for Saving Fuel," March 4, 1976.

LES GAPAY, "Distant Glimmer: Huge Power Stations for Solar Electricity Are Decades in Future," May 28, 1976.

184   MATERIALS MANAGEMENT

PETER R. KANN, "The Food Crisis: 'Green Revolution' Is Easing Hunger Slower Than Had Been Hoped," November 18, 1974.

BARRY KRAMER, "Ancient Enemy: Droughts May Spread in Big Climatic Shift, Some Studies Indicate," May 30, 1974.

BARRY KRAMER, "The Future Revised: Wiser Way of Living, Not Dramatic 'Cures,' Seen as Key to Health," March 22, 1976.

RICHARD J. LEVINE, "The Future Revised: Conventional Warfare Changing Faster Than the Experts Predicted," April 15, 1976.

JOAN LIBMAN and HERBERT LAWSON, "The Future Revised: The Family, Troubled by Changing Mores, Still Likely to Thrive," March 18, 1976.

JOANN S. LUBLIN, "The Man's Turn: Scientists Foresee Likely Development of Male Contraceptive," September 29, 1975.

ALFRED L. MALABRE, JR., "The Future Revised: U.S. Unlikely to Be as Big—or as Rich—as Analysts Thought," March 15, 1976.

R. MARTIN and R. J. MCCARTNEY, "The Future Revised: Education's Big Boom Is Ending, but Studies to Get More Diverse," April 8, 1976.

GAY SANDS MILLER, "Testing the Metal: Foreign-Supply Fears Spur Search in Industry for Alternate Materials," April 2, 1976.

DONALD MOFFITT, "Explosion in Energy, Technology Costs Has Changed the Shape of the Future," March 15, 1976.

ROGER RICKLEFS, "The Future Revised: Cities May Flourish in South and West, Decline in Northeast," April 6, 1976.

JONATHAN SPIVAK, "The Future Revised: Population of World Growing Faster Than Experts Anticipated," April 12, 1976.

JEFFREY A. TANNENBAUM, "Energy Alchemy: Researchers Say Sugar Made From Cellulose May One Day Provide New Food, Fuel Source," February 13, 1975.

JAMES TANNER, "The Future Revised: No Crippling Shortage of Energy Expected, but Cost Will Be High," March 29, 1976.

MIKE THARP, "Improved Image: Women in Work Force Post Better Records for Stability in Jobs," November 20, 1974.

MIKE THARP, "Last Minority? With Little Fanfare, More Firms Accept Homosexual Employees," July 1, 1974.

RAY VICKER, "The Food Crisis: Population Growth Is Still a Key Problem in Many Poor Nations," October 23, 1974.

JOSEPH M. WINSKI, "The Future Revised: By 2000, Prevention of Starvation May Be Chief Global Concern," March 25, 1976.

JOSEPH M. WINSKI, "New Way of Life? Back-to-Basics Trend in U.S. Eating Habits Appears Entrenched," May 29, 1975.